Acclaim for

ITALO CALVINO's

SIX MEMOS
for the
NEXT MILLENNIUM

"A brilliant, original approach to literature, a key to Calvino's own work and a thoroughly delightful and illuminating commentary on some of the world's greatest writing." — *San Francisco Chronicle*

"While [Calvino]'s loss is cause for universal mourning, his many books...call anew for celebration."
— *The New York Review of Books*

"[*Six Memos for the Next Millennium* is] a last exhortation, an encouragement to would-be creators of literature to digest the rules of survival Calvino has given them."
— *The Economist*

"These brilliant lectures, or 'memos,' are at once an intellectual dance and a description of the qualities that make Calvino's fiction so readable and so satisfying."
— *Boston Globe*

"As close as we'll ever get to the intellectual autobiography of a writer whose significance seems likely to last well into that coming millennium he addresses so warmly in these lectures."   — *Wall Street Journal*

ITALO CALVINO
SIX MEMOS
for the
NEXT MILLENNIUM

Italo Calvino (1923–1985) was born in Cuba and grew up in San Remo, Italy. He was a member of the partisan movement during the German occupation of northern Italy in World War II. The novel that resulted from that experience, published in English as *The Path to the Nest of Spiders,* won widespread acclaim. His other works of fiction include *The Baron in the Trees, The Castle of Crossed Destinies, Cosmicomics, Difficult Loves, If On a Winter's Night a Traveler, Invisible Cities, Marcovaldo, Mr. Palomar, The Nonexistent Knight and the Cloven Viscount, t zero, Under the Jaguar Sun,* and *The Watcher and Other Stories.* His works of nonfiction include *Six Memos for the Next Millennium* and *The Uses of Literature*, collections of literary essays, and the anthologies *Italian Folktales* and *Fantastical Tales.*

INTERNATIONAL

ALSO BY **ITALO CALVINO**

SIX MEMOS for the
NEXT MILLENNIUM

The Charles Eliot Norton Lectures
1985–86

SIX
MEMOS
for the
NEXT
MILLENNIUM

ITALO
CALVINO

Vintage International

VINTAGE BOOKS

A DIVISION OF RANDOM HOUSE, INC.

NEW YORK

FIRST VINTAGE INTERNATIONAL EDITION, SEPTEMBER 1993

Library of Congress Cataloging-in-Publication Data
Calvino, Italo.
    [Essays.   English.   Selections]
        Six memos for the next millennium / Italo Calvino. — 1st Vintage international ed.
        p.   cm.
    Collects five of six lectures Italo Calvino was about to deliver at the time of his death in 1985.
    Originally published: Cambridge, Mass.: Harvard University Press, 1988.
    ISBN 0-679-74237-9
    1. Literature — Philosophy.   2. Style, Literary.   3. Literature — History and criticism.   I. Title.
PN45.C3313   1993
801 — dc20   92-50641
                    CIP

Manufactured in the United States of America
B987654321

About the title: Although I carefully considered
the fact that the title chosen by Italo Calvino,
"Six Memos for the Next Millennium," does not
correspond to the manuscript as I found it, I have
felt it necessary to keep it. Calvino was delighted
by the word "memos," after having thought of
and dismissed titles such as "Some Literary Values," "A Choice of Literary Values," "Six Literary
Legacies"—all of them ending with "for the Next
Millennium."

Calvino started thinking about the Charles
Eliot Norton Lectures as soon as they were proposed in 1984. He stood before the vast range of
possibilities open to him and he worried, believ-
ing as he did in the importance of constraints,
until the day he settled on a scheme to organize
the lectures; after that, he devoted most of his
time to their preparation. From the first of January 1985 he did practically nothing else. They
became an obsession, and one day he announced
to me that he had ideas and material for *eight* lectures. I know the title for what might have been
an eighth lecture: "Sul cominciare e sul finire"
(On the beginning and the ending [of novels]).
But I have not yet been able to find the text.

My husband had finished writing these five
lectures by September 1985, at the moment of
departure for the United States and Harvard
University. Of course, these are the lectures
Calvino would have read—Patrick Creagh was in the
process of translating them—and he would certainly
have revised them before their publication as a
book by Harvard University Press. But I do not
think there would have been major changes:

the difference between the first versions I read and the final ones lies in structure, not content. Calvino wanted to call the sixth lecture "Consistency," and he planned to write it in Cambridge. I found the others, all in perfect order, in the Italian original, on his writing desk ready to be put into his suitcase.

I should like to express my gratitude to Patrick Creagh for his hard work on the translation; to Kathryn Hume, from Pennsylvania State University, for the help she has given me—in more ways than one—in preparing the manuscript for publication; and to Luca Marighetti, from Konstanz University, for his deep knowledge of Calvino's work and thought.

Esther Calvino

CONTENTS

SIX MEMOS
FOR THE NEXT MILLENNIUM

1 - Lightness

2 - Quickness

3 - Exactitude

4 - Visibility

5 - Multiplicity

6 - Consistency

We are in 1985, and barely fifteen years stand between us and a new millennium. For the time being I don't think the approach of this date arouses any special emotion. However, I'm not here to talk of futurology, but of literature. The millennium about to end has seen the birth and development of the modern languages of the West, and of the literatures that have explored the expressive, cognitive, and imaginative possibilities of these languages. It has also been the millennium of the book, in that it has seen the object we call a book take on the form now familiar to us. Perhaps it is a sign of our millennium's end that we frequently wonder what will happen to literature and books in the so-called postindustrial era of technology. I don't much feel like indulging in this sort of speculation. My confidence in the future of literature consists in the knowledge that there are things that only literature can give us, by means specific to it. I would therefore like to devote these lectures to certain values, qualities, or peculiarities of literature that are very close to my heart, trying to situate them within the perspective of the new millennium.

1

LIGHTNESS

I will devote my first lecture to the opposition between lightness and weight, and will uphold the values of lightness. This does not mean that I consider the virtues of weight any less compelling, but simply that I have more to say about lightness.

After forty years of writing fiction, after exploring various roads and making diverse experiments, the time has come for me to look for an overall definition of my work. I would suggest this: my working method has more often than not involved the subtraction of weight. I have tried to remove weight, sometimes from people, sometimes from heavenly bodies, sometimes from cities; above all I have tried to remove weight from the structure of stories and from language.

In this talk I shall try to explain—both to myself and to you— why I have come to consider lightness a value rather than a defect; to indicate the works of the past in which I recognize my ideal of lightness; and to show where I situate this value in the present and how I project it into the future.

I will start with the last point. When I began my career, the categorical imperative of every young writer was to represent his own time. Full of good intentions, I tried to identify myself with the ruthless energies propelling the events of our century, both collective and individual. I tried to find some harmony between the adventurous, picaresque inner rhythm that prompted me to write and the frantic spectacle of the world, sometimes dramatic and sometimes grotesque. Soon I became aware that between the facts of life that should have been my raw materials and the quick light touch I wanted for my writing, there was a gulf that cost me increasing effort to cross. Maybe I was only then becoming aware of the weight, the inertia, the opacity of the world—qualities that stick to writing from the start, unless one finds some way of evading them.

At certain moments I felt that the entire world was turning into stone: a slow petrification, more or less advanced depending on people and places but one that spared no aspect of life. It was as if no one could escape the inexorable stare of Medusa. The only hero able to cut off Medusa's head is Perseus, who flies with winged sandals; Perseus, who does not turn his gaze upon the face of the Gorgon but only upon her image reflected in his bronze shield. Thus Perseus comes to my aid even at this moment, just as I too am about to be caught in a vise of stone—which happens every time I try to speak about my own past. Better to let my talk be composed of images from mythology.

To cut off Medusa's head without being turned to stone, Perseus supports himself on the very lightest of things, the winds and the clouds, and fixes his gaze upon what can be revealed only by indirect vision, an image caught in a mirror. I am immediately tempted to see this myth as an allegory on the poet's relationship to the world, a lesson in the method to follow when writing. But I know that any interpretation impoverishes the myth and suffocates it. With myths, one should not be in a hurry. It is better to let them settle into the memory, to stop and dwell on every detail, to reflect on them without losing touch with their language of images. The lesson we can learn from a myth lies in the literal narrative, not in what we add to it from the outside.

The relationship between Perseus and the Gorgon is a complex one and does not end with the beheading of the monster. Medusa's blood gives birth to a winged horse, Pegasus—the heaviness of stone is transformed into its opposite. With one blow of his hoof on Mount Helicon, Pegasus makes a spring gush forth, where the Muses drink. In certain versions of the myth, it is Perseus who rides the miraculous Pegasus, so dear to the Muses, born from the accursed blood of Medusa. (Even the winged sandals, incidentally, come from the world of monsters, for Perseus obtained them from Medusa's sisters, the Graiae, who had one tooth and one eye among them.) As for the severed head, Perseus does not abandon it but carries it concealed in a bag. When his enemies are about to overcome him, he has only to display it, holding it by its snaky locks, and this bloodstained booty becomes an invincible weapon in the hero's hand. It is a weapon he uses only in cases of dire necessity, and only against those who deserve the punishment of being turned into statues. Here, certainly, the myth is telling us something, something implicit in the images that can't be explained in any other way. Perseus succeeds in mastering that horrendous face by keeping it hidden, just as in the first place he vanquished it by viewing it in a mirror. Perseus's strength always lies in a refusal to look directly, but not in a refusal of the reality in which he is fated to live; he carries the reality with him and accepts it as his particular burden.

On the relationship between Perseus and Medusa, we can learn something more from Ovid's *Metamorphoses*. Perseus wins another battle: he hacks a sea-monster to pieces with his sword and sets Andromeda free. Now he prepares to do what any of us would do after such an awful chore—he wants to wash his hands. But another problem arises: where to put Medusa's head. And here Ovid has some lines (IV.740–752) that seem to me extraordinary in showing how much delicacy of spirit a man must have to be a Perseus, killer of monsters: "So that the rough sand should not harm the snake-haired head (*anquiferumque caput dura ne laedat harena*), he makes the ground soft with a bed of leaves, and on top of that he strews little branches of plants born under water, and on this he places Medusa's head, face down." I think that the lightness, of which Perseus is the hero, could not be better represented than by this gesture of refreshing courtesy toward a being so monstrous and terrifying yet at the same time somehow fragile and perishable. But the most unexpected thing is the miracle that follows: when they touch Medusa, the little marine plants turn into coral and the nymphs, in order to have coral for adornments, rush to bring sprigs and seaweed to the terrible head.

This clash of images, in which the fine grace of the coral touches the savage horror of the Gorgon, is so suggestive that I would not like to spoil it by attempting glosses or interpretations. What I *can* do is to compare Ovid's lines with those of a modern poet, Eugenio Montale, in his "Piccolo testamento," where we also find the subtlest of elements—they could stand as symbols of his poetry: "traccia madreperlacea di lumaca / o smeriglio di vetro calpestato" (mother-of-pearl trace of a snail / or mica of crushed glass)—put up against a fearful, hellish monster, a Lucifer with pitch-black wings who descends upon the cities of the West. Never as in this poem, written in 1953, did Montale evoke such an apocalyptic vision, yet it is those minute, luminous tracings that are placed in the foreground and set in contrast to dark catastrophe—"Conservane la cipria nello specchietto / quando spenta ogni lampada / la sardana si farà infernale" (Keep its ash in your compact / when every lamp is out / and the sardana becomes infernal). But how can we hope to save ourselves in that which is most fragile? Montale's poem is a profession of faith in the persistence of what seems most fated to perish, in the moral values invested in the most tenuous traces: "il tenue bagliore strofinato / laggiù non era quello d'un fiammifero" (the thin glimmer striking down there / wasn't that of a match).*

In order to talk about our own times I have gone the long way around, calling up Ovid's fragile Medusa and Montale's black Lucifer. It is hard for a novelist to give examples of his idea of lightness from the events of everyday life, without making them the unattainable object of an endless *quête*. This is what Milan Kundera has done with great clarity and immediacy. His novel *The Unbearable Lightness of Being* is in reality a bitter confirmation of the Ineluctable Weight of Living, not only in the situation of desperate and all-pervading oppression that has been the fate of his hapless country, but in a human condition common to us all, however infinitely more fortunate we may be. For Kundera the weight of living consists chiefly in constriction, in the dense net of public and private constrictions that enfolds us more and more closely. His novel shows us how everything we choose and value in life for its lightness soon reveals its true, unbearable weight. Perhaps only the liveliness and mobility of the intelligence escape this sentence—the very qualities with which this novel is written, and which belong to a world quite different from the one we live in.

Whenever humanity seems condemned to heaviness, I think I should fly like Perseus into a different space. I don't mean escaping into dreams or into the irrational. I mean that I have to change my approach, look at the world from a different perspective, with a different logic and with fresh methods of cognition and verification. The images of lightness that I seek should not fade away like dreams dissolved by the realities of present and future . . . . .

In the boundless universe of literature there are always new

---

*The English translation of these lines from Montale's "Little Testament" has been provided by Jonathan Galassi.

a sideways look

avenues to be explored, both very recent and very ancient, styles and forms that can change our image of the world . . . . . But if literature is not enough to assure me that I am not just chasing dreams, I look to science to nourish my visions in which all heaviness disappears. Today every branch of science seems intent on demonstrating that the world is supported by the most minute entities, such as the messages of DNA, the impulses of neurons, and quarks, and neutrinos wandering through space since the beginning of time . . . . .

Then we have computer science. It is true that software cannot exercise its powers of lightness except through the weight of hardware. But it is software that gives the orders, acting on the outside world and on machines that exist only as functions of software and evolve so that they can work out ever more complex programs. The second industrial revolution, unlike the first, does not present us with such crushing images as rolling mills and molten steel, but with "bits" in a flow of information traveling along circuits in the form of electronic impulses. The iron machines still exist, but they obey the orders of weightless bits.

Is it legitimate to turn to scientific discourse to find an image of the world that suits my view? If what I am attempting here attracts me, it is because I feel it might connect with a very old thread in the history of poetry.

The *De Rerum Natura* of Lucretius is the first great work of poetry in which knowledge of the world tends to dissolve the solidity of the world, leading to a perception of all that is infinitely minute, light, and mobile. Lucretius set out to write the poem of physical matter, but he warns us at the outset that this matter is made up of invisible particles. He is the poet of physical concreteness, viewed in its permanent and immutable substance, but the first thing he tells us is that emptiness is just as concrete as solid bodies. Lucretius' chief concern is to prevent

*a God of surpress
as a child I loved surps*

the weight of matter from crushing us. Even while laying down
the rigorous mechanical laws that determine every event, he
feels the need to allow atoms to make unpredictable deviations
from the straight line, thereby ensuring freedom both to atoms
and to human beings. The poetry of the invisible, of infinite unexpected possibilities—even the poetry of nothingness—issues
from a poet who had no doubts whatever about the physical
reality of the world.

This atomizing of things extends also to the visible aspects of
the world, and it is here that Lucretius is at his best as a poet:
the little motes of dust swirling in a shaft of sunlight in a dark
room (II.114-124); the minuscule shells, all similar but each one
different, that waves gently cast up on the *bibula harena,* the "im-
bibing sand" (II.374–376); or the spiderwebs that wrap themselves around us without our noticing them as we walk along
(III.381–390).

I have already mentioned Ovid's *Metamorphoses,* another encyclopedic poem (written fifty years after Lucretius'), which has its
starting point not in physical reality but in the fables of mythology. For Ovid, too, everything can be transformed into something else, and knowledge of the world means dissolving the solidity of the world. And also for him there is an essential parity
between everything that exists, as opposed to any sort of hierarchy of powers or values. If the world of Lucretius is composed
of immutable atoms, Ovid's world is made up of the qualities,
attributes and forms that define the variety of things, whether
plants, animals, or persons. But these are only the outward appearances of a single common substance that—if stirred by profound emotion—may be changed into what most differs from it.

It is in following the continuity of the passage from one form
to another that Ovid displays his incomparable gifts. He tells how
a woman realizes that she is changing into a lotus tree: her feet

are rooted to the earth, a soft bark creeps up little by little and enfolds her groin; she makes a movement to tear her hair and finds her hands full of leaves. Or he speaks of Arachne's fingers, expert at winding or unraveling wool, turning the spindle, plying the needle in embroidery, fingers that at a certain point we see lengthening into slender spiders' legs and beginning to weave a web.

In both Lucretius and Ovid, lightness is a way of looking at the world based on philosophy and science: the doctrines of Epicurus for Lucretius and those of Pythagoras for Ovid (a Pythagoras who, as presented by Ovid, greatly resembles the Buddha). In both cases the lightness is also something arising from the writing itself, from the poet's own linguistic power, quite independent of whatever philosophic doctrine the poet claims to be following.

From what I have said so far, I think the concept of lightness is beginning to take shape. Above all I hope to have shown that there is such a thing as a lightness of thoughtfulness, just as we all know that there is a lightness of frivolity. In fact, thoughtful lightness can make frivolity seem dull and heavy.

I could not illustrate this notion better than by using a story from the *Decameron* (VI.9), in which the Florentine poet Guido Cavalcanti appears. Boccaccio presents Cavalcanti as an austere philosopher, walking meditatively among marble tombs near a church. The *jeunesse dorée* of Florence is riding through the city in a group, on the way from one party to another, always looking for a chance to enlarge its round of invitations. Cavalcanti is not popular with them because, although wealthy and elegant, he has refused to join in their revels—and also because his mysterious philosophy is suspected of impiety.

Ora avvenne un giorno che, essendo Guido partito d'Orto San Michele e venutosene per lo Corso degli Adimari infino a San Giovanni, il quale spesse volte era suo cammino, essendo arche grandi di marmo, che oggi sono in Santa Reparata, e molte altre dintorno a San Giovanni, e egli essendo tralle colonne del porfido che vi sono e quelle arche e la porta di San Giovanni, che serrata era, messer Betto con sua brigata a caval venendo su per la piazza di Santa Reparata, vedendo Guido là tra quelle sepolture, dissero: "Andiamo a dargli briga"; e spronati i cavalli, a guisa d'uno assalto sollazzevole gli furono, quasi prima che egli se ne avvedesse, sopra e cominciarongli a dire: "Guido, tu rifiuti d'esser di nostra brigata; ma ecco, quando tu avrai trovato che Idio non sia, che avrai fatto?"

A' quali Guido, da lor veggendosi chiuso, prestamente disse: "Signori, voi mi potete dire a casa vostra ciò che vi piace"; e posta la mano sopra una di quelle arche, che grandi erano, sí come colui che leggerissimo era, prese un salto e fusi gittato dall'altra parte, e sviluppatosi da loro se n'andò.

One day, Guido left Orto San Michele and walked along the Corso degli Adimari, which was often his route, as far as San Giovanni. Great marble tombs, now in Santa Reparata, were then scattered about San Giovanni. As he was standing between the porphyry columns of the church and these tombs, with the door of the church shut fast behind him, Messer Betto and his company came riding along the Piazza di Santa Reparata. Catching sight of Guido among the tombs, they said, "Let's go and pick a quarrel." Spurring their horses, they came down upon him in play, like a charging squad, before he was aware of them. They began:

"Guido, you refuse to be of our company; but look, when you have proved that there is no God, what will you have accomplished?" Guido, seeing himself surrounded by them, answered quickly: "Gentlemen, you may say anything you wish to me in your own home." Then, resting his hand on one of the great tombs and being very nimble, he leaped over it and, landing on the other side, made off and rid himself of them.

What interests us here is not so much the spirited reply attributed to Cavalcanti (which may be interpreted in the light of the fact that the "Epicurianism" claimed by the poet was really Averroism, according to which the individual soul is only a part of the universal intellect: the tombs are *your* home and not mine insofar as individual bodily death is overcome by anyone who rises to universal contemplation through intellectual speculation). What strikes me most is the visual scene evoked by Boccaccio, of Cavalcanti freeing himself with a leap "sí come colui che leggerissimo era," a man very light in body.

Were I to choose an auspicious image for the new millennium, I would choose that one: the sudden agile leap of the poet-philosopher who raises himself above the weight of the world, showing that with all his gravity he has the secret of lightness, and that what many consider to be the vitality of the times— noisy, aggressive, revving and roaring—belongs to the realm of death, like a cemetery for rusty old cars.

I would like you to bear this image in mind as I proceed to talk about Cavalcanti as the poet of lightness. The dramatis personae of his poems are not so much human beings as sighs, rays of light, optical images, and above all those nonmaterial impulses and messages he calls "spirits." A theme by no means "light," such as the sufferings of love, is dissolved into impalpable entities that move between sensitive soul and intellective soul, between heart and mind, between eyes and voice. In short, in every case we are concerned with something marked by three characteristics: (1) it is to the highest degree light; (2) it is in motion; (3) it is a vector of information. In some poems this messenger-cum-message is the poetic text itself. In the most famous one—"Per ch'i' no spero di tornai giammai" (Because I never hope to return)—the exiled poet addresses the ballad he is writing and says: "Va' tu, leggera e piana, / dritt' a la donna mia" (Go, light and soft, / straight to my lady). In another poem it is the tools of the writer's trade—quills and the knives to sharpen them—that have their say: "Noi siàn le triste penne isbigottite / le cesoiuzze e'l coltellin dolente" (We are the poor, bewildered quills, / The little scissors and the grieving penknife). In sonnet 13 the word "spirito" or "spiritello" appears in every line. In what is plainly a self-parody, Cavalcanti takes his predilection for that key word to its ultimate conclusion, concentrating a complicated abstract narrative involving fourteen "spirits," each with a different function, and all within the scope of fourteen lines. In another sonnet the body is dismembered by the sufferings of love, but goes on walking about like an automaton "fatto di rame o di pietra o di legno" (made of copper or stone or wood). Years before, Guinizelli in one of his sonnets had transformed his poet into a brass statue, a concrete image that draws its strength from the very sense of weight it communicates. In Cavalcanti the weight of matter is dissolved because the materials of the human simulacrum can be many, all interchangeable. The metaphor does not impress a solid image on us, and not even the word *pietra* (stone) lends heaviness to the line. Here also we find the equality of all existing things that I spoke of in regard to Lucretius and Ovid. The critic Gianfranco Contini defines it as the "parificazione cavalcantiana dei reali," referring to Cavalcanti's way of putting everything on the same level.

The most felicitous example of Cavalcanti's leveling of things we find in a sonnet that begins with a list of images of beauty, all destined to be surpassed by the beauty of the beloved woman:

> Biltà di donna e di saccente core
> e cavalieri armati che sien genti;
> cantar d'augelli e ragionar d'amore;
> adorni legni 'n mar forte correnti;
>
> aria serena quand'apar l'albore
> e bianca neve scender senza venti;
> rivera d'acqua e prato d'ogni fiore;
> oro, argento, azzuro 'n ornamenti

Beauty of woman and of wise hearts, and gentle knights in armor; the song of birds and the discourse of love; bright ships moving swiftly on the sea; clear air when the dawn appears, and white snow falling without wind; stream of water and meadow with every flower; gold, silver, azure in ornaments.

The line "e bianca neve scender senza venti" is taken up with a few modifications by Dante in *Inferno* XIV.30: "Come di neve in alpe sanza vento" (As snow falls in the mountains without wind). The two lines are almost identical, but they express two completely different concepts. In both the snow on windless days suggests a light, silent movement. But here the resemblance ends. In Dante the line is dominated by the specification of the place ("in alpe"), which gives us a mountainous landscape, whereas in Cavalcanti the adjective "bianca," which may seem pleonastic, together with the verb "fall"—also completely predictable—dissolve the landscape into an atmosphere of suspended abstraction. But it is chiefly the first word that determines the difference between the two lines. In Cavalcanti the conjunction *e* (and) puts the snow on the same level as the other visions that precede and follow it: a series of images like a catalogue of the beauties of the world. In Dante the adverb *come* (as) encloses the entire scene in the frame of a metaphor, but within this frame it has a concrete reality of its own. No less concrete and dramatic is the landscape of hell under a rain of fire, which he illustrates by the simile of the snow. In Cavalcanti everything moves so swiftly that we are unaware of its consistency, only of its effects. In Dante everything acquires consistency and stability: the weight of things is precisely established. Even when he is speaking of light things, Dante seems to want to render the exact weight of this lightness: "come di neve in alpe sanza vento." In another very similar line the weight of a body sinking into the water and disappearing is, as it were, held back and slowed down: "Come per acqua cupa cosa grave" (Like some heavy thing in deep water; *Paradiso* III.123).

At this point we should remember that the idea of the world as composed of weightless atoms is striking just because we know the weight of things so well. So, too, we would be unable to appreciate the lightness of language if we could not appreciate language that has some weight to it.

We might say that throughout the centuries two opposite tendencies have competed in literature: one tries to make language into a weightless element that hovers above things like a cloud or better, perhaps, the finest dust or, better still, a field of magnetic impulses. The other tries to give language the weight, density, and concreteness of things, bodies, and sensations.

At the very beginnings of Italian, and indeed European, literature, the first tendency was initiated by Cavalcanti, the second by Dante. The contrast is generally valid but would need endless qualification, given Dante's enormous wealth of resources and his extraordinary versatility. It is not by chance that the sonnet of

Dante's instilled with the most felicitous lightness ("Guido, i'
vorrei che tu e Lapo ed io") is in fact addressed to Cavalcanti. In
the *Vita nuova* Dante deals with the same material as his friend
and master, and certain words, themes, and ideas are found in
both poets. When Dante wants to express lightness, even in the
Divina Commedia, no one can do it better than he does, but his
real genius lies in the opposite direction—in extracting all the
possibilities of sound and emotion and feeling from the language,
in capturing the world in verse at all its various levels, in all its
forms and attributes, in transmitting the sense that the world is
organized into a system, an order, or a hierarchy where everything has its place. To push this contrast perhaps too far, I might
say that Dante gives solidity even to the most abstract intellectual
speculation, whereas Cavalcanti dissolves the concreteness of
tangible experience in lines of measured rhythm, syllable by syllable, as if thought were darting out of darkness in swift lightning
flashes.

This discussion of Cavalcanti has served to clarify (at least to
myself) what I mean by "lightness." Lightness for me goes with
precision and determination, not with vagueness and the hap-
hazard. Paul Valéry said: "Il faut être léger comme l'oiseau, et
non comme la plume" (One should be light like a bird, and not
like a feather). I have relied on Cavalcanti for examples of lightness in at least three different senses. First there is a lightening
of language whereby meaning is conveyed through a verbal texture that seems weightless, until the meaning itself takes on the
same rarefied consistency. I leave it to you to find other examples
of this sort. Emily Dickinson, for instance, can supply as many as
we might wish:

> A sepal, petal and a thorn
> Upon a common summer's morn—

A flask of Dew—A Bee or two—
A Breeze—a caper in the trees—
And I'm a Rose!

Second, there is the narration of a train of thought or psychological process in which subtle and imperceptible elements are at work, or any kind of description that involves a high degree of abstraction. To find a more modern example of this we may turn to Henry James, opening any of his books at random:

It was as if these depths, constantly bridged over by a structure that was firm enough in spite of its lightness and of its occasional oscillation in the somewhat vertiginous air, invited on occasion, in the interest of their nerves, a dropping of the plummet and a measurement of the abyss. A difference had been made moreover, once for all, by the fact that she had, all the while, not appeared to feel the need of rebutting his charge of an idea within her that she didn't dare to express, uttered just before one of the fullest of their later discussions ended. ("The Beast in the Jungle," chap. 3)

And third there is a visual image of lightness that acquires emblematic value, such as—in Boccaccio's story—Cavalcanti vaulting on nimble legs over a tombstone. Some literary inventions are impressed on our memories by their verbal implications rather than by their actual words. The scene in which Don Quixote drives his lance through the sail of a windmill and is hoisted up into the air takes only a few lines in Cervantes' novel. One might even say that the author put only a minimal fraction of his resources into the passage. In spite of this, it remains one of the most famous passages in all of literature.

I think that with these definitions I can begin to leaf through the books in my library, seeking examples of lightness. In Shakespeare I look immediately for the point at which Mercutio arrives on the scene (I.iv.17–18): "You are a lover; borrow Cupid's wings / And soar with them above a common bound." Mercutio immediately contradicts Romeo, who has just replied, "Under love's heavy burden do I sink." Mercutio's way of moving about the world is plain enough from the very first verbs he uses: to dance, to soar, to prick. The human face is a mask, "a visor." Scarcely has he come on stage when he feels the need to explain his philosophy, not with a theoretical discourse but by relating a dream. Queen Mab, the fairies' midwife, appears in a chariot made of "an empty hazelnut":

> Her wagon-spokes made of long spinners' legs,
> The cover, of the wings of grasshoppers;
> Her traces, of the smallest spider web;
> Her collars, of the moonshine's wat'ry beams;
> Her whip, of cricket's bone; the lash, of film

And let's not forget that this coach is "drawn with a team of little atomies"—in my opinion a vital detail that enables the dream of Queen Mab to combine Lucretian atomism, Renaissance neo-Platonism, and Celtic folklore.

I would also like Mercutio's dancing gait to come along with us across the threshold of the new millennium. The times that form a background to *Romeo and Juliet* are in many respects not unlike our own: cities bloodstained by violent struggles just as senseless as those of the Montagues and Capulets; sexual liberation, as preached by the Nurse, which does not succeed in becoming the model for universal love; ventures carried out in the generous optimism of "natural philosophy," as preached by Friar Laurence, with unsure results that can yield death as much as life.

The age of Shakespeare recognized subtle forces connecting macrocosm and microcosm, ranging from those of the Neo-Platonic firmament to the spirits of metal transformed in the alchemist's crucible. Classical myths can provide their repertory of nymphs and dryads, but the Celtic mythologies are even richer in the imagery of the most delicate natural forces, with their elves and fairies. This cultural background—and I can't help thinking of Francis Yates's fascinating studies on the occult philosophy of the Renaissance and its echoes in literature—explains why Shakespeare provides the fullest exemplification of my thesis. And I am not thinking solely of Puck and the whole phantasmagoria of *A Midsummer Night's Dream* or of Ariel and those who "are such stuff / As dreams are made on." I am thinking above all of that particular and existential inflection that makes it possible for Shakespeare's characters to distance themselves from their own drama, thus dissolving it into melancholy and irony.

The weightless gravity I have spoken of with regard to Cavalcanti reappears in the age of Cervantes and Shakespeare: it is that special connection between melancholy and humor studied by Raymond Klibansky, Erwin Panofsky, and Fritz Saxl in *Saturn and Melancholy* (1964). As melancholy is sadness that has taken on lightness, so humor is comedy that has lost its bodily weight (a dimension of human carnality that nonetheless constitutes the greatness of Boccaccio and Rabelais). It casts doubt on the self, on the world, and on the whole network of relationships that are at stake. Melancholy and humor, inextricably intermingled, characterize the accents of the Prince of Denmark, accents we have learned to recognize in nearly all Shakespeare's plays on the lips of so many avatars of Hamlet. One of these, Jacques in *As You Like It* (IV.i.15–18), defines melancholy in these terms: "but it is a melancholy of mine own, compounded of many simples, extracted from many objects, and indeed the sundry contemplation of my travels, which, by often rumination, wraps me in a most humorous sadness." It is therefore not a dense, opaque melancholy, but a veil of minute particles of humours and sensations, a fine dust of atoms, like everything else that goes to make up the ultimate substance of the multiplicity of things.

I confess that I am tempted to construct my own Shakespeare, a Lucretian atomist, but I realize that this would be arbitrary. The first writer in the modern world who explicitly professed an atomistic concept of the universe in its fantastic transfiguration is not found until some years later, in France: Cyrano de Bergerac.

An extraordinary writer, Cyrano, and one who deserves to be better known, not only as the first true forerunner of science fiction but for his intellectual and poetic qualities. A follower of Gassendi's "sensism" and the astronomy of Copernicus, but nourished above all by the natural philosophy of the Italian Renaissance—Cardano, Bruno, Campanella—Cyrano is the first poet of atomism in modern literature. In pages where his irony cannot conceal a genuine cosmic excitement, Cyrano extols the unity of all things, animate or inanimate, the combinatoria of elementary figures that determine the variety of living forms; and above all he conveys his sense of the precariousness of the processes behind them. That is, how nearly man missed being man, and life, life, and the world, the world.

> Vous vous étonnez comme cette matière, brouillée pêle-mêle, au gré du hasard, peut avoir constitué un homme, vu qu'il y avait tant de choses nécessaires à la construction de son être, mais vous ne savez pas que cent millions de fois cette matière, s'acheminant au dessein d'un homme, s'est

arrêtée à former tantôt une pierre, tantôt du plomb, tantôt du corail, tantôt une fleur, tantôt une comète, pour le trop ou le trop peu de certaines figures qu'il fallait ou ne fallait pas à désigner un homme? Si bien que ce n'est pas merveille qu'entre une infinie quantité de matière qui change et se remue incessamment, elle ait rencontré à faire le peu d'animaux, de végétaux, de minéraux que nous voyons; non plus que ce n'est pas merveille qu'en cent coups de dés il arrive un rafle. Aussi bien est-il impossible que de ce remuement il ne se fasse quelque chose, et cette chose sera toujours admirée d'un étourdi qui ne saura pas combien peu s'en est fallu qu'elle n'ait pas été faite. (*Voyage dans la lune,* 1661, Garnier-Flammarion edition, pp. 98–99)

You marvel that this matter, shuffled pell-mell at the whim of Chance, could have made a man, seeing that so much was needed for the construction of his being. But you must realize that a hundred million times this matter, on the way to human shape, has been stopped to form now a stone, now lead, now coral, now a flower, now a comet; and all because of more or fewer elements that were or were not necessary for designing a man. Little wonder if, within an infinite quantity of matter that ceaselessly changes and stirs, the few animals, vegetables, and minerals we see should happen to be made; no more wonder than getting a royal pair in a hundred casts of the dice. Indeed it is equally impossible for all this stirring not to lead to something; and yet this something will always be wondered at by some blockhead who will never realize how small a change would have made it into something else.

By this route Cyrano goes so far as to proclaim the brotherhood of men and cabbages, and thus imagines the protest of a cabbage about to be beheaded: "Homme, mon cher frère, que t'ai-je fait qui mérite la mort? . . . Je me lève de terre, je m'épan-ouis, je te tends les bras, je t'offre mes enfants en graine, et pour récompense de ma courtoisie, tu me fais trancher la tête!" (Man, my dear brother, what have I done to you, to deserve death? . . . I rise from the earth, I blossom forth, I stretch out my arms to you, I offer you my children as seed; and as a reward for my courtesy you have my head cut off!).

If we consider that this peroration in favor of truly universal *fraternité* was written nearly one hundred and fifty years before the French revolution, we see how the sluggishness of the human consciousness in emerging from its anthropocentric parochialism can be abolished in an instant by poetic invention. And all this in the context of a trip to the moon, in which Cyrano's imagination outdistances his most illustrious predecessors, Lucian of Samosata and Ludovico Ariosto. In my discussion of lightness, Cyrano is bound to figure chiefly because of the way in which (before Newton) he felt the problem of universal gravitation. Or, rather, it is the problem of escaping the force of gravity that so stimulates his imagination as to lead him to think up a whole series of ways of reaching the moon, each one more ingenious than the last—for example, by using a phial filled with dew that evaporates in the sun; by smearing himself with ox marrow, which is usually sucked up by the moon; or by repeatedly tossing up a magnetized ball from a little boat.

As for the technique of magnetism, this was destined to be developed and perfected by Jonathan Swift to keep the flying island of Laputa in the air. The moment at which Laputa first appears in flight is one when Swift's two obsessions seem to cancel out in an instant of magical equilibrium. I am speaking of the bodiless abstraction of the rationalism at which his satire is aimed and the material weight of the body: "and I could see the sides of it, encompassed with several gradations of galleries, and stairs at certain intervals, to descend from one to the other. In the lowest gallery I beheld some people fishing with long angling rods, and others looking on." Swift was a contemporary and adversary of Newton. Voltaire was an admirer of Newton, and he imagined a giant called Micromégas, who in contrast to Swift's giants is defined not by his bulk but by dimensions expressed in figures, by spatial and temporal properties enumerated in the rigorous, impassive terms of scientific treatises. In virtue of this logic and style, Micromégas succeeds in flying through space from Sirius to Saturn to Earth. One might say that, in Newton's theories, what most strikes the literary imagination is not the conditioning of everything and everyone by the inevitability of its own weight, but rather the balance of forces that enables heavenly bodies to float in space.

The eighteenth-century imagination is full of figures suspended in air. It is no accident that at the beginning of that century Antoine Galland's French translation of the *Thousand and One Nights* opened up the imagination of the West to the Eastern sense of marvel: flying carpets, winged horses, genies emerging from lamps. In this drive to make the imagination exceed all bounds, the eighteenth century reached its climax with the flight of Baron von Münchausen on a cannonball, an image identified forever in our minds with the illustrations that are Gustave Doré's masterpiece. These adventures of Münchausen, which—like the *Thousand and One Nights*—may have had one author, many authors, or none at all, are a constant challenge to the laws of gravity. The baron is carried aloft by ducks; he pulls up himself and his horse by tugging at the pigtail of his wig; he comes down from the moon on a rope that during the descent is several times cut and reknotted.

These images from folk literature, along with those we have

seen from more learned literature, are part of the literary reper-
cussions of Newton's theories. When he was fifteen years old,
Giacomo Leopardi wrote an amazingly erudite *History of Astronomy,* in which among other things he sums up Newton's theories.
The gazing at the night skies that inspires Leopardi's most beautiful lines was not simply a lyrical theme: when he spoke about
the moon, Leopardi knew exactly what he was talking about. In
his ceaseless discourses on the unbearable weight of living, Leopardi bestows many images of lightness on the happiness he
thinks we can never attain: birds, the voice of a girl singing at a
window, the clarity of the air—and, above all, the moon.

As soon as the moon appears in poetry, it brings with it a
sensation of lightness, suspension, a silent calm enchantment.
When I began thinking about these lectures, I wanted to devote
one whole talk to the moon, to trace its apparitions in the literatures of many times and places. Then I decided that the moon
should be left entirely to Leopardi. For the miraculous thing
about his poetry is that he simply takes the weight out of language, to the point that it resembles moonlight. The appearances
of the moon in his poetry do not take up many lines, but they
are enough to shed the light of the moon on the whole poem, or
else to project upon it the shadow of its absence.

> Dolce e chiara è la notte e senza vento
> e queta sovra i tetti e in mezzo agli orti
> posa la luna, e di lontan rivela
> serena ogni montagna.
>   ·   ·   ·   ·   ·
> O graziosa luna, io mi rammento
> che, or volge l'anno, sovra questo colle
> io venia pien d'angoscia a rimirarti:
> e tu pendevi allor su quella selva
> siccome fai, che tutta la rischiari.

. . . . .

O cara luna, al cui tranquillo raggio
danzan le lepri nelle selve . . .

. . . . .

Già tutta l'aria imbruna,
torna azzurro il sereno, e tornan l'ombre
giù da' colli e da' tetti,
al biancheggiar della recente luna.

. . . . .

Che fai tu, luna, in ciel? Dimmi, che fai,
silenziosa luna?
Sorgi la sera e vai,
contemplando i deserti, indi ti posi.

Soft and clear is the night and without wind, and quietly
over the roofs and in the gardens rests the moon, and far
away reveals every peaceful mountain.

. . . . .

O gentle, gracious moon, I remember now, it must be a
year ago, on this same hill I came to see you; I was full of
sorrow. And you were leaning then above that wood just as
now, filling it all with brilliance.

. . . . .

O cherished moon, beneath whose quiet beams the hares
dance in the woods . . .

. . . . .

Already all the air darkens, deepens to blue, and shadows glide
from roofs and hills at the whitening of the recent moon.

. . . . .

What do you do there, moon, in the sky? Tell me what you
do, silent moon. When evening comes you rise and go contemplating wastelands; then you set.

Have a great number of threads been interwoven in this lecture? Which thread should I pull on to find the end in my hand? There is the thread that connects the moon, Leopardi, Newton, gravitation and levitation. There is the thread of Lucretius, atomism, Cavalcanti's philosophy of love, Renaissance magic, Cyrano. Then there is the thread of writing as a metaphor of the powder-fine substance of the world. For Lucretius, letters were atoms in continual motion, creating the most diverse words and sounds by means of their permutations. This notion was taken up by a long tradition of thinkers for whom the world's secrets were contained in the combinatoria of the signs used in writing: one thinks of the *Ars Magna* of Raymond Lully, the Cabala of the Spanish rabbis and of Pico della Mirandola . . . . . Even Galileo saw the alphabet as the model for all combinations of minimal units . . . . . And then Leibniz . . . . .

Should I continue along this road? Won't the conclusions awaiting me seem all too obvious? Writing as a model for every process of reality . . . . . indeed the only reality we can know, indeed the only reality *tout court* . . . . . No, I will not travel such roads as these, for they would carry me too far from the use of words as I understand it—that is, words as a perpetual pursuit of things, as a perpetual adjustment to their infinite variety.

There remains one thread, the one I first started to unwind: that of literature as an existential function, the search for lightness as a reaction to the weight of living. Perhaps even Lucretius was moved by this need, perhaps even Ovid: Lucretius who was seeking—or thought he was seeking—Epicurean impassiveness; and Ovid who was seeking—or thought he was seeking—reincarnation in other lives according to the teachings of Pythagoras.

I am accustomed to consider literature a search for knowledge. In order to move onto existential ground, I have to think of literature as extended to anthropology and ethnology and mythology. Faced with the precarious existence of tribal life—drought, sickness, evil influences—the shaman responded by ridding his body of weight and flying to another world, another level of perception, where he could find the strength to change the face of reality. In centuries and civilizations closer to us, in villages where the women bore most of the weight of a constricted life, witches flew by night on broomsticks or even on lighter vehicles such as ears of wheat or pieces of straw. Before being codified by the Inquisition, these visions were part of the folk imagination, or we might even say of lived experience. I find it a steady feature in anthropology, this link between the levitation desired and the privation actually suffered. It is this anthropological device that literature perpetuates.

First, oral literature: in folktales a flight to another world is a common occurrence. Among the "functions" catalogued by Vladimir Propp in his *Morphology of the Folktale* (1968), it is one of the methods of "transference of the hero," defined as follows: "Usually the object sought is in 'another' or 'different' realm that may be situated far away horizontally, or else at a great vertical depth or height." Propp then goes on to list a great number of examples of the hero flying through the air: on horseback or on the back of a bird, disguised as a bird, in a flying boat, on a flying carpet, on the shoulders of a giant or a spirit, in the devil's wagon.

It is probably not pushing things too far to connect the functions of shamanism and witchcraft documented in ethnology and folklore with the catalogue of images contained in literature. On the contrary, I think that the deepest rationality behind every literary operation has to be sought out in the anthropological needs to which it corresponds.

I would like to end this talk by mentioning Kafka's "Der Kübelreiter" (The Knight of the Bucket). This is a very short story written in 1917 in the first person, and its point of departure is plainly a real situation in that winter of warfare, the worst for the Austrian Empire: the lack of coal. The narrator goes out with an empty bucket to find coal for the stove. Along the way the bucket serves him as a horse, and indeed it takes him up as far as the second floor of a house, where he rocks up and down as if riding on the back of a camel. The coal merchant's shop is underground, and the bucket rider is too high up. He has a hard time getting his message across to the man, who would really like to respond to his request, but the coal merchant's wife wants nothing to do with him. He begs them to give him a shovelful of even the worst coal, even though he can't pay immediately. The coal merchant's wife unties her apron and shooes away the intruder as if he were a fly. The bucket is so light that it flies off with its rider until it disappears beyond the Ice Mountains.

Many of Kafka's short stories are mysterious, and this one is particularly so. It may be that Kafka only wanted to tell us that going out to look for a bit of coal on a cold wartime night changes the mere swinging of an empty bucket into the quest of a knight-errant or the desert crossing of a caravan or a flight on a magic carpet. But the idea of an empty bucket raising you above the level where one finds both the help and the egoism of others; the empty bucket, symbol of privation and desire and seeking, raising you to the point at which a humble request can no longer be satisfied—all this opens the road to endless reflection.

I have spoken of the shaman and the folktale hero, of privation that is transformed into lightness and makes possible a flight into a realm where every need is magically fulfilled. I have spoken of witches flying on humble household implements, such as a bucket. But the hero of Kafka's story doesn't seem to be endowed with the powers of shamanism or witchcraft; nor does the country beyond the Ice Mountains seem to be one in which the empty bucket will find anything to fill it. In fact, the fuller it is, the less it will be able to fly. Thus, astride our bucket, we shall face the new millennium, without hoping to find anything more in it than what we ourselves are able to bring to it. Lightness, for example, whose virtues I have tried to illustrate here.

2

QUICKNESS

I will start by telling you an ancient legend.

Late in life the emperor Charlemagne fell in love with a German girl. The barons at his court were extremely worried when they saw that the sovereign, wholly taken up with his amorous passion and unmindful of his regal dignity, was neglecting the affairs of state. When the girl suddenly died, the courtiers were greatly relieved—but not for long, because Charlemagne's love did not die with her. The emperor had the embalmed body carried to his bedchamber, where he refused to be parted from it. The Archbishop Turpin, alarmed by this macabre passion, suspected an enchantment and insisted on examining the corpse. Hidden under the girl's dead tongue he found a ring with a precious stone set in it. As soon as the ring was in Turpin's hands, Charlemagne fell passionately in love with the archbishop and hurriedly had the girl buried. In order to escape the embarrassing situation, Turpin flung the ring into Lake Constance. Charlemagne thereupon fell in love with the lake and would not leave its shores.

This legend, "taken from a book on magic," is set down even more concisely than I have recorded it in a book of unpublished notes by the French Romantic writer Jules Barbey d'Aurevilly (you can find it in the notes to the Pléiade edition of Barbey d'Aurevilly's works, I.1315). Ever since I read it, the legend has kept coming back into my mind as if the spell of the ring were continuing to act through the medium of the story.

Let me try to explain why such a story can be so fascinating to us. What we have is a series of totally abnormal events linked together: the love of an old man for a young girl, a necrophiliac obsession and a homosexual impulse, while in the end everything subsides into melancholy contemplation, with the old king staring in rapture at the lake. "Charlemagne, la vue attachée sur son lac de Constance, amoureux de l'abîme caché" (Charlemagne, his eyes fixed on Lake Constance, in love with the hidden abyss), writes Barbey d'Aurevilly in the passage in his novel (*Une vieille maîtresse*, p. 221) which he annotates by relating the legend.

To hold this chain of events together, there is a verbal link, the word "love" or "passion," which establishes a continuity between different forms of attraction. There is also a narrative link, the magic ring that establishes a logical relationship of cause and effect between the various episodes. The drive of desire toward a thing that does not exist, a lack or absence symbolized by the empty circle of the ring, is expressed more by the rhythm of the story than by the events narrated. In the same way, the whole story is shot through with a sense of death, against which Charlemagne appears to be struggling feverishly by clinging to the last remnants of life; a fever that then subsides in the contemplation of the lake.

The real protagonist of the story, however, is the magic ring, because it is the movements of the ring that determine those of the characters and because it is the ring that establishes the relationships between them. Around the magic object there forms a kind of force field that is in fact the territory of the story itself. We might say that the magic object is an outward and visible sign that reveals the connection between people or between events. It has a narrative function, whose history we may trace in the

Norse sagas and the chivalric romances—a function that continues to surface in Italian poems of the Renaissance. In Ariosto's
Orlando furioso we find an endless series of exchanges of swords,
shields, helmets, and horses, each one endowed with particular
qualities. In this way the plot can be described in terms of the
changes of ownership of a certain number of objects, each one
endowed with certain powers that determine the relationships
between certain characters.

In realistic narrative, Mambrino's helmet becomes a barber's
bowl, but it does not lose importance or meaning. In the same
way, enormous weight is attached to all the objects that Robinson
Crusoe saves from the wrecked ship or makes with his own
hands. I would say that the moment an object appears in a narrative, it is charged with a special force and becomes like the pole
of a magnetic field, a knot in the network of invisible relationships. The symbolism of an object may be more or less explicit,
but it is always there. We might even say that in a narrative any
object is always magic.

Returning to the Charlemagne legend, we find it has a literary
tradition in Italian. In his *Lettere famigliari* (I.4) Petrarch tells us
that he had heard this "not unpleasant tale" (*fabella non ina-
mena*)—which he says he doesn't believe—while visiting Charlemagne's tomb at Aix-la-Chapelle. In Petrarch's Latin, the story is
much richer in moral comment, and also in detail and feeling
(the bishop of Cologne, in obedience to a miraculous voice from
heaven, gropes with his finger beneath the cold, rigid tongue of
the corpse: *sub gelida rigentique lingua*). But speaking for myself, I
greatly prefer the bare résumé, in which everything is left to the
imagination and the speed with which events follow one another
conveys a feeling of the ineluctable.

The legend reappears in the flowery language of sixteenth-
century Italy in various versions, in which the necrophiliac aspect

acquires the most emphasis. Sebastiano Erizzo, a Venetian writer of novellas, puts into the mouth of Charlemagne—while he is in bed with the corpse—a lamentation several pages in length. On the other hand, the homosexual aspect of the emperor's passion for the archbishop is hardly ever alluded to, or even expunged altogether, as in one of the most famous sixteenth-century treatises on love (that of Giuseppe Bettussi) in which the story ends with the finding of the ring. As for the ending, in Petrarch and his Italian followers, Lake Constance is not mentioned because the entire action takes place at Aix-la-Chapelle, since the legend was supposed to be an explanation of the origins of the palace and the church the emperor had built there. The ring is thrown into a marsh, whose muddy stench the emperor breathes in as if it were perfume, while "he takes delight in using its waters." Here there is a link with other local legends on the origins of the thermal springs, details that put even more emphasis on the mortuary quality of the whole affair.

Even earlier than this were the German medieval traditions studied by Gaston Paris. These deal with Charlemagne's love for a dead woman with variants that make it a very different story. Now the belovèd is the emperor's legal wife, who uses the magic ring to ensure his fidelity; at other times she is a fairy or nymph who dies when the ring is taken from her; sometimes she is a woman who seems to be alive but is discovered to be a corpse once the ring is removed. At the bottom of all this there may well be a Scandinavian saga: Harald, king of Norway, slept with his dead wife who was wrapped in a magic cloak that gave her the appearance of being alive.

In a word, in the medieval versions collected by Gaston Paris, what is lacking is the chain of events; in the literary versions of Petrarch and the Renaissance writers, what is missing is speed. So I still prefer the version given by Barbey d'Aurevilly, in spite of its rather patched-up crudity. The secret of the story lies in its economy: the events, however long they last, become puncti-form, connected by rectilinear segments, in a zigzag pattern that suggests incessant motion.

I do not wish to say that quickness is a value in itself. Narrative time can also be delaying, cyclic, or motionless. In any case, a story is an operation carried out on the length of time involved, an enchantment that acts on the passing of time, either contract-ing or dilating it. Sicilian storytellers use the formula "lu cuntu nun metti tempu" (time takes no time in a story) when they want to leave out links or indicate gaps of months or even years. The technique of oral narration in the popular tradition follows functional criteria. It leaves out unnecessary details but stresses repetition: for example, when the tale consists of a series of the same obstacles to be overcome by different people. A child's plea-sure in listening to stories lies partly in waiting for things he expects to be repeated: situations, phrases, formulas. Just as in poems and songs the rhymes help to create the rhythm, so in prose narrative there are events that rhyme. The Charlemagne legend is highly effective narrative because it is a series of events that echo each other as rhymes do in a poem.

If during a certain period of my career as a writer I was at-tracted by folktales and fairytales, this was not the result of loy-alty to an ethnic tradition (seeing that my roots are planted in an entirely modern and cosmopolitan Italy), nor the result of nos-talgia for things I read as a child (in my family, a child could read only educational books, particularly those with some scientific basis). It was rather because of my interest in style and structure, in the economy, rhythm, and hard logic with which they are told. In working on my transcription of Italian folktales as recorded by scholars of the last century, I found most enjoyment when the original text was extremely laconic. This I tried to convey, respecting the conciseness and at the same time trying to obtain the greatest possible narrative force. See, for instance, number 57 in *Italian Folktales (Fiabe italiane):*

> Un Re s'ammalò. Vennero i medici e gli dissero: "Senta, Maestà, se vuol guarire, bisogna che lei prenda una penna dell'Orco. E' un rimedio difficile, perchè l'Orco tutti i cristiani che vede se li mangia.
>
> Il Re lo disse a tutti ma nessuno ci voleva andare. Lo chiese a un suo sottoposto, molto fedele e coraggioso, e questi disse: "Andrò."
>
> Gli insegnarono la strada: "In cima a un monte, ci sono sette buche: in una delle sette, ci sta l'Orco."
>
> L'uomo andò e lo prese il buio per la strada. Si fermò in una locanda . . .

> A king fell ill and was told by his doctors, "Majesty, if you want to get well, you'll have to obtain one of the ogre's feathers. That will not be easy, since the ogre eats every human he sees."
>
> The king passed the word on to everybody, but no one was willing to go to the ogre. Then he asked one of his most loyal and courageous attendants, who said, "I will go."
>
> The man was shown the road and told, "On a mountaintop are seven caves, in one of which lives the ogre."
>
> The man set out and walked until dark, when he stopped at an inn . . . *

Not a word is said about what illness the king was suffering from, or why on earth an ogre should have feathers, or what

---

* "The Feathered Ogre," translated by George Martin, from *Italian Folktales* (New York: Harcourt Brace Jovanovich, 1956, 1980).

those caves were like. But everything mentioned has a necessary function in the plot. The very first characteristic of a folktale is economy of expression. The most outlandish adventures are recounted with an eye fixed on the bare essentials. There is always a battle against time, against the obstacles that prevent or delay the fulfillment of a desire or the repossession of something cherished but lost. Or time can stop altogether, as in the castle of Sleeping Beauty. To bring this about, Charles Perrault has only to write: "Les broches mêmes qui étaient au feu toutes pleines de perdrix et de faisans s'endormirent, et le feu aussi. Tout cela se fit en un moment; les Fées n'étaient pas longues à leur besogne" (Even the spits on the fire, all laden with partridges and pheasants, went to sleep, and the fire along with them. All this happened in a moment: the fairies were not long at their work).

The relativity of time is the subject of a folktale known almost everywhere: a journey to another world is made by someone who thinks it has lasted only a few hours, though when he returns, his village is unrecognizable because years and years have gone by. In early American literature, of course, this was the theme of Washington Irving's "Rip Van Winkle," which acquired the status of a foundation myth for your ever-changing society.

This motif can also be interpreted as an allegory of narrative time and the way in which it cannot be measured against real time. And the same significance can be seen in the reverse operation, in the expanding of time by the internal proliferations from one story to another, which is a feature of oriental storytelling. Scheherazade tells a story in which someone tells a story in which someone tells a story, and so forth. The art that enables Scheherazade to save her life every night consists of knowing how to join one story to another, breaking off at just the right moment—two ways of manipulating the continuity and discontinuity of time. It is a secret of rhythm, a way of capturing time that we can recognize from the very beginning: in the epic by means of the metrical effects of the verse, in prose narrative by those effects that make us eager to know what comes next.

Everybody knows the discomfort felt when someone sets out to tell a joke without being good at it and gets everything wrong, by which I mean, above all, the links and the rhythms. This feeling is evoked in one of Boccaccio's novellas (VI.1), which is in fact devoted to the art of storytelling.

A jovial company of ladies and gentlemen, guests of a Florentine lady in her country house, go for an after-lunch outing to another pleasant place in the neighborhood. To cheer them on their way, one of the men offers to tell a story.

"Madonna Oretta, quando voi vogliate, io vi porterò, gran parte della via che a andare abbiamo, a cavallo con una delle belle novelle del mondo."

Al quale la donna rispuose: "Messere, anzi ve ne priego io molto, e sarammi carissimo."

Messer lo cavaliere, al quale forse non stava meglio la spada allato che 'l novellar nella lingua, udito questo, cominciò una sua novella, la quale nel vero da sé era bellissima, ma egli or tre e quatro e sei volte replicando una medesima parola e ora indietro tornando e talvolta dicendo: "Io non dissi bene" e spesso ne' nomi errando, un per un altro ponendone, fieramente la guastava: senza che egli pessimamente, secondo le qualità delle persone e gli atti che accadevano, profereva.

Di che a madonna Oretta, udendolo, spesse volte veniva un sudore e uno sfinimento di cuore, come se inferma fosse stata per terminare; la qual cosa poi che piú sofferir non poté, conoscendo che il cavaliere era entrato nel pecoreccio né era per riuscirne, piacevolmente disse: "Messer, questo vostro cavallo ha troppo duro trotto, per che io vi priego che vi piaccia di pormi a piè."

"Mistress Oretta, if you please, I shall carry you a great part of the way we have to go on horseback, with one of the best stories in the world." "Sir," she replied, "I pray you to do so; that will be most agreeable." Hearing this, master cavalier, who perhaps fared no better with sword at side than with tale on tongue, began his story, which was indeed a very fine one. But what with his repeating of the same word three or four or six times over, his recapitulations, his "I didn't say that right," his erring in putting one name for another, he spoiled it dreadfully. Also his delivery was very poor, quite out of keeping with the circumstances and the quality of his persons. Mistress Oretta, hearing him, was many times taken with a sweat and a sinking of the heart, as if she were sick and about to die. At last, unable to endure the torment any longer and seeing that the gentleman was entangled in a maze of his own making, she said pleasantly: "Sir, this horse of yours has too hard a trot, and I pray you to set me on my feet again."

The novella is a horse, a means of transport with its own pace, a trot or a gallop according to the distance and the ground it has to travel over; but the speed Boccaccio is talking about is a mental speed. The listed defects of the clumsy storyteller are above all offenses against rhythm, as well as being defects of style, because he does not use the expressions appropriate either to the characters or to the events. In other words, even correctness of style is a question of quick adjustment, of agility of both thought and expression.

The horse as an emblem of speed, even speed of the mind, runs through the whole history of literature, heralding the entire problematics of our own technological viewpoint. The age of speed, in transport as in information, opens with one of the finest essays in English literature, Thomas De Quincey's "The English Mail-Coach." In 1849 he already understood everything we now know about the motorized highway world, including death-dealing high-speed crashes.

In the section called "The Vision of Sudden Death," De Quincey describes a night journey on the box of an express mail coach with a gigantic coachman who is fast asleep. The technical perfection of the vehicle, and the transformation of the driver into a blind inanimate object, puts the traveler at the mercy of the mechanical inexorability of a machine. In the clarity of perception brought on by a dose of laudanum, De Quincey becomes aware that the horses are running uncontrollably at thirteen miles an hour on the wrong side of the road. This means certain disaster, not for the swift, sturdy mail coach but for the first unfortunate carriage to come along that road in the opposite direction. In fact, at the end of the straight, tree-lined avenue, which looks like a "Gothic aisle," he sees a "frail reedy gig" in which a young couple are approaching at one mile an hour. "Between them and eternity, to all human calculation, there is but a minute and a-half." De Quincey gives a shout: "Mine had been the first step; the second was for the young man; the third was for God." The account of these few seconds has not been bettered even in an age in which the experience of high speeds has become a basic fact of life.

> Glance of eye, thought of man, wing of angel, which of these had speed enough to sweep between the question and the answer, and divide the one from the other? Light does not tread upon the steps of light more indivisibly than did our all-conquering arrival upon the escaping efforts of the gig.

De Quincey succeeds in conveying a sense of an extremely short period of time that nonetheless contains both the calculation of the technical inevitability of the crash and the imponderable—God's part in the matter—in virtue of which the two vehicles do not collide.

The motif that interests us here is not physical speed, but the relationship between physical speed and speed of mind. This was also interesting to a great Italian poet of De Quincey's generation. Giacomo Leopardi, whose youth was as sedentary as one can imagine, struck a rare joyful moment when he wrote in his diary, the *Zibaldone di pensieri* (Casual Thoughts):

> La velocità, per esempio, de' cavalli o veduta, o sperimentata, cioè quando essi vi trasportano . . . è piacevolissima per se sola, cioè per la vivacità, l'energia, la forza, la vita di tal sensazione. Essa desta realmente una quasi idea dell' infinito, sublima l'anima, la fortifica . . . (27 Ottobre 1821).

> Speed, for example, of horses, whether seen or experienced, that is, when they are carrying you . . . is most pleasurable in itself; that is, for the vivacity, the energy, the strength, the sheer life of such a feeling. Indeed it almost gives you an idea of the infinite—elevates the soul, fortifies it.

In his notes in the *Zibaldone* over the following few months, Leopardi develops his reflections on the subject of speed, and at a certain point starts to speak about literary style:

> La rapidità e la concisione dello stile, piace perchè presenta all'anima una folla d'idee simultanee, o così rapidamente succedentisi, che paiono simultanee, e fanno ondeggiar l'anima in una tale abbondanza di pensieri, o d'immagini e sensazioni spirituali, ch'ella o non è capace di abbracciarle

tutte, e pienamente ciascuna, o non ha tempo di restare in ozio, e priva di sensazioni. La forza dello stile poetico, che in gran parte è tutt'uno colla rapidità, non è piacevole per altro che per questi effetti, e non consiste in altro. L'eccitamento d'idee simultanee, può derivare e da ciascuna parola isolata, o propria o metaforica, e dalla loro collocazione, e dal giro della frase, e dalla soppressione stessa di altre parole o frasi ec. (3 Novembre 1821).

Speed and conciseness of style please us because they present the mind with a rush of ideas that are simultaneous, or that follow each other so quickly they seem simultaneous, and set the mind afloat on such an abundance of thoughts or images or spiritual feelings that either it cannot embrace them all, each one fully, or it has no time to be idle and empty of feelings. The power of poetic style, which is largely the same thing as rapidity, is pleasing for these effects alone and consists in nothing else. The excitement of simultaneous ideas may arise either from each isolated word, whether literal or metaphorical, from their arrangement, from the turn of a phrase, or even from the suppression of other words and phrases.

The metaphor of the horse for the speed of thought was, I think, first used by Galileo Galilei. In the *Saggiatore* (The Tester), arguing with an adversary who propped up his own theories with a vast number of classical quotations, he wrote:

Se il discorrere circa un problema difficile fosse come il portar pesi, dove molti cavalli porteranno più sacca di grano che un caval solo, io acconsentirei che i molti discorsi facesser più che un solo; ma il discorrere è come il correre, e non come il portare, ed un caval barbero solo correrà più che cento frisoni. (45)

> If discoursing on a difficult problem were like carrying weights, when many horses can carry more sacks of grain than a single horse, I would agree that many discourses would do more than a single one; but discoursing is like coursing, not like carrying, and one Barbary courser can go faster than a hundred Frieslands.

"Discoursing," or "discourse," for Galileo means reasoning, and very often deductive reasoning. "Discoursing is like coursing": this statement could be Galileo's declaration of faith—style as a method of thought and as literary taste. For him, good thinking means quickness, agility in reasoning, economy in argument, but also the use of imaginative examples.

There is also a certain predilection for the horse in Galileo's metaphors and *Gedanken-Experimenten*. In a study I once made on metaphor in Galileo, I counted at least eleven significant examples in which he talks of horses—as an image of motion, and therefore as an instrument in kinetic experiments; as a form of nature in all its complexity and also in all its beauty; as a form that sparks off the imagination in the hypothetical situation of horses subjected to the most unlikely trials or growing to gigantic proportions—and all this apart from the comparison of reasoning with racing: "Discoursing is like coursing."

In the *Dialogo dei massimi sistemi* (Dialogue Concerning the Two Chief World Systems), speed of thought is personified by Sagredo, a character who intervenes in the discussion between the Ptolomaic Simplicio and the Copernican Salviati. Salviati and Sagredo represent two different facets of Galileo's temperament. Salviati is the rigorously methodical reasoner, who proceeds slowly and with prudence; Sagredo, with his "swift manner of speech" and more imaginative way of seeing things, draws conclusions that have not been demonstrated and pushes every idea to its extreme consequences. It is Sagredo who makes hypotheses on how life might be on the moon or what would happen if the earth stopped turning. But it is Salviati who defines the scale of values in which Galileo places quickness of mind. Instantaneous reasoning without *passaggi* (transitions) is the reasoning of God's mind, infinitely superior to the mind of man, which however should not be despised or considered nothing, insofar as it was created by God, and in the course of time has investigated and understood and achieved wonderful things. At this point Sagredo breaks in with an encomium on the greatest human invention, the alphabet:

> Ma sopra tutte le invenzioni stupende, qual eminenza di mente fu quella di colui che s'immaginò di trovar modo di comunicare i suoi più reconditi pensieri a qualsivoglia altra persona, benchè distante per lunghissimo intervallo di luogo e di tempo? parlare con quelli che son nell'Indie, parlare a que li che non sono ancora nati né saranno se non di qua a mille e dieci mila anni? e con qual facilità? con i vari accozzamenti di venti caratteruzzi sopra una carta. (End of the first day)

> But above all stupendous inventions, what eminence of mind was his who dreamed of finding means to communicate his deepest thoughts to any other person, no matter how far distant in place and time? Of speaking with those who are in India, of speaking with those who are not yet born and will not be born for a thousand or ten thousand years? And with what facility? All by using the various arrangements of twenty little characters on a page!

In my last talk, on lightness, I quoted Lucretius, who in the combinatoria of the alphabet saw a model of the impalpable atomic structure of matter. Now I quote Galileo who, in the combinatoria of the alphabet ("the various arrangements of twenty little characters on a page"), saw the ultimate instrument of communication. Communication with people distant in place and time, says Galileo; but we should also add the immediate connection that writing establishes between everything existent or possible.

Since in each of my lectures I have set myself the task of recommending to the next millennium a particular value close to my heart, the value I want to recommend today is precisely this: In an age when other fantastically speedy, widespread media are triumphing, and running the risk of flattening all communication onto a single, homogeneous surface, the function of literature is communication between things that are different simply because they are different, not blunting but even sharpening the differences between them, following the true bent of written language.

The motor age has forced speed on us as a measurable quantity, the records of which are milestones in the history of the progress of both men and machines. But mental speed cannot be measured and does not allow comparisons or competitions; nor can it display its results in a historical perspective. Mental speed is valuable for its own sake, for the pleasure it gives to anyone who is sensitive to such a thing, and not for the practical use that can be made of it. A swift piece of reasoning is not necessarily better than a long-pondered one. Far from it. But it communicates something special that is derived simply from its very swiftness.

I said at the beginning that each value or virtue I chose as the subject for my lectures does not exclude its opposite. Implicit in my tribute to lightness was my respect for weight, and so this apologia for quickness does not presume to deny the pleasures of lingering. Literature has worked out various techniques for slowing down the course of time. I have already mentioned repetition, and now I will say a word about digression.

In practical life, time is a form of wealth with which we are stingy. In literature, time is a form of wealth to be spent at leisure and with detachment. We do not have to be first past a predetermined finish line. On the contrary, saving time is a good thing because the more time we save, the more we can afford to lose. Quickness of style and thought means above all agility, mobility, and ease, all qualities that go with writing where it is natural to digress, to jump from one subject to another, to lose the thread a hundred times and find it again after a hundred more twists and turns.

Laurence Sterne's great invention was the novel that is completely composed of digressions, an example followed by Diderot. The digression is a strategy for putting off the ending, a multiplying of time within the work, a perpetual evasion or flight. Flight from what? From death, of course, says Carlo Levi, in an introduction he wrote to an Italian edition of *Tristram Shandy*. Few people would imagine Levi to be an admirer of Sterne, but actually his own secret lay precisely in bringing a spirit of digression and a feeling of unlimited time even to the observation of social problems. Levi writes:

> L'orologio è il primo simbolo di Shandy. Sotto il suo influsso egli viene generato, ed iniziano le sue disgrazie, che sono tutt'uno con questo segno del tempo. La morte sta nascosta negli orologi, come diceva il Belli; e l'infelicità della vita individuale, di questo frammento, di questa cosa scissa e disgregata, e priva di totalità: la morte, che è il tempo, il

tempo della individuazione, della separazione, l'astratto tempo che rotola verso la sua fine. Tristram Shandy non vuol nascere, perchè non vuol morire. Tutti i mezzi, tutte le armi sono buone per salvarsi dalla morte e dal tempo. Se la linea retta è la più breve fra due punti fatali e inevitabili, le digressioni la allungheranno: e se queste digressioni diventeranno così complesse, aggrovigliate, tortuose, così rapide da far perdere le proprie tracce, chissà che la morte non ci trovi più, che il tempo si smarrisca, e che possiamo restare celati nei mutevoli nascondigli.

The clock is Shandy's first symbol. Under its influence he is conceived and his misfortunes begin, which are one and the same with this emblem of time. Death is hidden in clocks, as Belli said; and the unhappiness of individual life, of this fragment, of this divided, disunited thing, devoid of wholeness: death, which is time, the time of individuation, of separation, the abstract time that rolls toward its end. Tristram Shandy does not want to be born, because he does not want to die. Every means and every weapon is valid to save oneself from death and time. If a straight line is the shortest distance between two fated and inevitable points, digressions will lengthen it; and if these digressions become so complex, so tangled and tortuous, so rapid as to hide their own tracks, who knows—perhaps death may not find us, perhaps time will lose its way, and perhaps we ourselves can remain concealed in our shifting hiding places.

Words, words that make me think. Because I am not devoted to aimless wandering, I'd rather say that I prefer to entrust myself to the straight line, in the hope that the line will continue into infinity, making me unreachable. I prefer to calculate at length the trajectory of my flight, expecting that I will be able to launch myself like an arrow and disappear over the horizon. Or else, if too many obstacles bar my way, to calculate the series of rectilinear segments that will lead me out of the labyrinth as quickly as possible.

From my youth on, my personal motto has been the old Latin tag, *Festina lente,* hurry slowly. Perhaps what attracted me, even more than the words and the idea, was the suggestiveness of its emblems. You may recall that the great Venetian humanist publisher, Aldus Manutius, on all his title pages symbolized the motto *Festina lente* by a dolphin in a sinuous curve around an anchor. The intensity and constancy of intellectual work are represented in that elegant graphic trademark, which Erasmus of Rotterdam commented on in some memorable pages. But both dolphin and anchor belong to the same world of marine emblems, and I have always preferred emblems that throw together incongruous and enigmatic figures, as in a rebus. Such are the butterfly and crab that illustrate *Festina lente* in the sixteenth-century collection of emblems by Paolo Giovio. Butterfly and crab are both bizarre, both symmetrical in shape, and between them establish an unexpected kind of harmony.

My work as a writer has from the beginning aimed at tracing the lightning flashes of the mental circuits that capture and link points distant from each other in space and time. In my love of adventure stories and fairytales, I have always searched for the equivalent of some inner energy, some motion of the mind. I have always aimed at the image and the motion that arises naturally from the image, while still being aware that one cannot speak of a literary result until this stream of imagination has been turned into words. Just as for the poet writing verse, so it is for the prose writer: success consists in felicity of verbal expression, which every so often may result from a quick flash of inspiration but as a rule involves a patient search for the *mot juste,* for the sentence in which every word is unalterable, the most effective marriage of sounds and concepts. I am convinced that writing prose should not be any different from writing poetry. In both cases it is a question of looking for the unique expression, one that is concise, concentrated, and memorable.

It is hard to keep up tension of this kind in very long works. However, by temperament I feel myself more at ease in short pieces: much of my work consists of short stories. For example, the sort of thing I tried out in *Cosmicomics (Le cosmicomiche)* and *t zero (T con zero)*—giving narrative form to abstract ideas of space and time—could not be brought off except within the brief span of a short story. But I have experimented with even shorter compositions, with narrative on a smaller scale, something between a fable and a *petit poème en prose,* in my book *Invisible Cities (Le città invisibili)* and more recently in my descriptions in *Palomar*. Of course the length or brevity of a text is an external criterion, but I am speaking of a particular density that, even if it can be attained in narratives of broader scope, nevertheless finds its proper dimension in the single page.

In this preference for short literary forms I am only following the true vocation of Italian literature, which is poor in novelists but rich in poets, who even when they write in prose give of their best in texts where the highest degree of invention and thought is contained in a few pages. This is the case with a book unparalleled in other literatures: Leopardi's *Operette morali* (Essays and Dialogues). American literature has a glorious and thriving tradition of short stories, and indeed I would say that its most precious gems are to be found there. But the rigid distinction made by publishers—either short story or novel—excludes other possible short forms (which still may be found in the prose works of the great American poets, from Walt Whitman's *Specimen Days* to many pages of William Carlos Williams). The demands of the publishing business are a fetish that must not be allowed to keep us from trying out new forms. I should like at this point to break a lance on the field for the richness of short literary forms, with all they imply in terms of style and concentration of content. I am thinking of the Paul Valéry of *Monsieur Teste* and many of his essays, of the prose poems that Francis Ponge wrote about objects, of Michel Leiris' explorations of himself and his own language, of Henri Michaux's mysterious and hallucinatory humor in the very brief stories in *Plume*.

The last great invention of a new literary genre in our time was achieved by a master of the short form, Jorge Luis Borges. It was the invention of himself as narrator, that "Columbus' egg," which enabled him to get over the mental block that until nearly forty years of age prevented him from moving beyond essays to fiction. The idea that came to Borges was to pretend that the book he wanted to write had already been written by someone else, some unknown hypothetical author—an author in a different language, of a different culture—and that his task was to describe and review this invented book. Part of the Borges legend is the anecdote that when the first extraordinary story written according to this formula, "El acercamiento a Almotásim" (The Approach to Al'Mutásim), appeared in the magazine *Sur* in 1940, it was in fact believed to be a review of a book by an Indian author. In the same way, critics of Borges feel bound to observe that each of his texts doubles or multiplies its own space through the medium of other books belonging to a real or imaginary library, whether they be classical, erudite, or merely invented.

What I particularly wish to stress is how Borges achieves his approaches to the infinite without the least congestion, in the most crystalline, sober, and airy style. In the same way, his synthetic, sidelong manner of narration brings with it a language that is everywhere concrete and precise, whose inventiveness is shown in the variety of rhythms, the syntactic movements, the unfailingly surprising and unexpected adjectives. Borges has created a literature raised to the second power and, at the same time, a literature that is like the extraction of the square root of itself. It is a "potential literature," to use a term applied later on in France. The first signs of this may be found in *Ficciones,* in the little hints and formulas of what might have become the works of a hypothetical author called Herbert Quain.

Conciseness is only one aspect of the subject I want to deal with, and I will confine myself to telling you that I dream of immense cosmologies, sagas, and epics all reduced to the dimensions of an epigram. In the even more congested times that await us, literature must aim at the maximum concentration of poetry and of thought.

Borges and Bioy Casares put together an anthology of short extraordinary tales (*Cuentos breves y extraordinarios,* 1955). I would like to edit a collection of tales consisting of one sentence only, or even a single line. But so far I haven't found any to match the one by the Guatemalan writer Augusto Monterroso: "Cuando despertó, el dinosauro todavía estaba allí" (When I woke up, the dinosaur was still there).

I realize that this talk, based as it is on invisible connections, has wandered off in many directions and is risking dispersion. But all the subjects I have dealt with this evening, and perhaps those from last time, might indeed be united in that they are all under the sign of an Olympian god whom I particularly honor: Hermes-Mercury, god of communication and mediation, who under the name of Thoth was the inventor of writing and who— according to C. G. Jung in his studies on alchemical symbolism— in the guise of "spirit Mercury" also represents the *principium individuationis.* Mercury with his winged feet, light and airborne, astute, agile, adaptable, free and easy, established the relationships of the gods among themselves and those between the gods and men, between universal laws and individual destinies, between the forces of nature and the forms of culture, between the objects of the world and all thinking subjects. What better patron could I possibly choose to support my proposals for literature?

For the ancients, who saw microcosm and macrocosm mirrored in the correspondences between psychology and astrology, between humours, temperaments, planets, and constellations, Mercury's nature was the most indefinite and variable. But, in the more widespread view, the temperament influenced by Mercury, inclined toward exchanges and commerce and dexterity, was contrasted with the temperament influenced by Saturn, seen as melancholy, contemplative, and solitary. Ever since antiquity it has been thought that the saturnine temperament is the one proper to artists, poets, and thinkers, and that seems true enough. Certainly literature would never have existed if some human beings had not been strongly inclined to introversion, discontented with the world as it is, inclined to forget themselves for hours and days on end and to fix their gaze on the immobility of silent words. Certainly my own character corresponds to the traditional features of the guild to which I belong. I too have always been saturnine, whatever other masks I have attempted to wear. My cult of Mercury is perhaps merely an aspiration, what I would like to be. I am a Saturn who dreams of being a Mercury, and everything I write reflects these two impulses.

But if Saturn-Chronos does exercise some power over me, it is also true that he is not one of my favorite divinities. I have never nourished any feeling for him other than a timorous respect. There is, however, another god with family ties to Saturn for whom I feel much affection. He is a god who does not enjoy too much astrological and therefore psychological prestige, since his name was not given to one of the seven planets in the skies of the ancients, but still he has been well treated in literature from Homer on. I am speaking of Vulcan–Hephaestus, a god who does not roam the heavens but lurks at the bottom of craters, shut up in his smithy, where he tirelessly forges objects that are the last word in refinement: jewels and ornaments for the gods and goddesses, weapons, shields, nets, traps. To Mercury's aerial flight, Vulcan replies with his limping gait and the rhythmic beat of his hammer.

Here too I have to refer to some occasional reading of mine— from time to time enlightening ideas emerge from reading odd books that are hard to classify from a rigorously academic point of view. The book in question, which I read while studying the symbolism of the tarot, is André Virel's *Histoire de nôtre image* (1965). According to the author—a student of the collective imagination in what I take to be the school of Jung—Mercury and Vulcan represent the two inseparable and complementary functions of life: Mercury represents *syntony,* or participation in the world around us; Vulcan, *focalization* or constructive concentration. Mercury and Vulcan are both sons of Jupiter, whose realm is that of the consciousness, individual and social. But on his mother's side Mercury is a descendant of Uranus, whose kingdom was that of the "cyclophrenic" age of undifferentiated continuity. And Vulcan is descended from Saturn, whose realm was that of the "schizophrenic" era of egocentric isolation. Saturn dethroned Uranus, and Jupiter dethroned Saturn. In the end, in the well-balanced, luminous realm of Jupiter, both Mercury and Vulcan carry with them the memory of some dark primordial realm, changing what had been a destructive malady into something positive: syntony and focalization.

Even since I read Virel's explanation of how Mercury and Vulcan are both contrasting and complementary, I have begun to understand something that I had only a rather vague idea of before—something about myself, about how I am and how I would like to be; about how I write and how I might be able to write. Vulcan's concentration and craftsmanship are needed to record Mercury's adventures and metamorphoses. Mercury's swiftness and mobility are needed to make Vulcan's endless labors become bearers of meaning. And from the formless mineral matrix, the gods' symbols of office acquire their forms: lyres or tridents, spears or diadems.

A writer's work has to take account of many rhythms: Vulcan's and Mercury's, a message of urgency obtained by dint of patient and meticulous adjustments and an intuition so instantaneous that, when formulated, it acquires the finality of something that could never have been otherwise. But it is also the rhythm of time that passes with no other aim than to let feelings and thoughts settle down, mature, and shed all impatience or ephemeral contingency.

I began this lecture by telling a story. Let me end it with another story, this time Chinese: Among Chuang-tzu's many skills, he was an expert draftsman. The king asked him to draw a crab. Chuang-tzu replied that he needed five years, a country house, and twelve servants. Five years later the drawing was still not begun. "I need another five years," said Chuang-tzu. The king granted them. At the end of these ten years, Chuang-tzu took up his brush and, in an instant, with a single stroke, he drew a crab, the most perfect crab ever seen.

3

EXACTITUDE

For the ancient Egyptians, exactitude was symbolized by a feather that served as a weight on scales used for the weighing of souls. This light feather was called Maat, goddess of the scales. The hieroglyph for Maat also stood for a unit of length—the 33 centimeters of the standard brick—and for the fundamental note of the flute.

This information comes from a lecture by Giorgio de Santillana on the precision of the ancients in observing astronomical phenomena, a lecture I heard in Italy in 1963 which had a profound influence on me. These days I have often thought of Santillana, who acted as my guide in Massachusetts during my first visit to the United States in 1960. In memory of his friendship, I have started this talk on exactitude in literature with the name of Maat, goddess of the scales—all the more because Libra is my sign of the Zodiac.

First I shall try to define my subject. To my mind exactitude means three things above all:

(1) a well-defined and well-calculated plan for the work in question;
(2) an evocation of clear, incisive, memorable visual images; in Italian we have an adjective that doesn't exist in English, "icastico," from the Greek εἰκαστικός;

(3) a language as precise as possible both in choice of words and in expression of the subtleties of thought and imagination.

Why do I feel the need to defend values that many people might take to be perfectly obvious? I think that my first impulse arises from a hypersensitivity or allergy. It seems to me that language is always used in a random, approximate, careless manner, and this distresses me unbearably. Please don't think that my reaction is the result of intolerance toward my neighbor: the worst discomfort of all comes from hearing myself speak. That's why I try to talk as little as possible. If I prefer writing, it is because I can revise each sentence until I reach the point where—if not exactly satisfied with my words—I am able at least to eliminate those reasons for dissatisfaction that I can put a finger on. Literature—and I mean the literature that matches up to these requirements—is the Promised Land in which language becomes what it really ought to be.

It sometimes seems to me that a pestilence has struck the human race in its most distinctive faculty—that is, the use of words. It is a plague afflicting language, revealing itself as a loss of cognition and immediacy, an automatism that tends to level out all expression into the most generic, anonymous, and abstract formulas, to dilute meanings, to blunt the edge of expressiveness, extinguishing the spark that shoots out from the collision of words and new circumstances.

At this point, I don't wish to dwell on the possible sources of this epidemic, whether they are to be sought in politics, ideology, bureaucratic uniformity, the monotony of the mass media, or the way the schools dispense the culture of the mediocre. What interests me are the possibilities of health. Literature, and perhaps literature alone, can create the antibodies to fight this plague in language.

I would like to add that it is not just language that seems to have been struck by this pestilence. Consider visual images, for example. We live in an unending rainfall of images. The most powerful media transform the world into images and multiply it by means of the phantasmagoric play of mirrors. These are images stripped of the inner inevitability that ought to mark every image as form and as meaning, as a claim on the attention and as a source of possible meanings. Much of this cloud of visual images fades at once, like the dreams that leave no trace in the memory, but what does not fade is a feeling of alienation and discomfort.

But maybe this lack of substance is not to be found in images or in language alone, but in the world itself. This plague strikes also at the lives of people and the history of nations. It makes all histories formless, random, confused, with neither beginning nor end. My discomfort arises from the loss of form that I notice in life, which I try to oppose with the only weapon I can think of—an idea of literature.

Therefore I can even use negative terms to define the values I am setting out to defend. It remains to be seen whether by using equally convincing arguments one cannot defend the contrary thesis. For example, Giacomo Leopardi maintained that the more vague and imprecise language is, the more poetic it becomes. I might mention in passing that as far as I know Italian is the only language in which the word *vago* (vague) also means "lovely, attractive." Starting out from the original meaning of "wandering," the word *vago* still carries an idea of movement and mutability, which in Italian is associated both with uncertainty and indefiniteness and with gracefulness and pleasure.

To put my cult of exactitude to the proof, I will look back at those pages of the *Zibaldone* where Leopardi praises *il vago*. He says: "Le parole *lontano, antico* e simili sono poeticissime e piacevoli, perchè destano idee vaste, e indefinite . . . (25 Settembre

1821)" (The words *lontano, antico* [faraway, ancient], and similar words are highly poetic and pleasurable because they evoke vast, indefinite ideas). "Le parole *notte, notturno* ec., le descrizioni della notte ec., sono poeticissime, perchè la notte confondendo gli oggetti, l'animo non ne concepisce che un'immagine vaga, indistinta, incompleta, sì di essa che quanto ella contiene. Così *oscurità, profondo* ec. ec. (28 Settembre 1821)" (The words *notte, notturno* [night, nocturnal], etc., descriptions of the night, etc., are highly poetic because, as night makes objects blurred, the mind receives only a vague, indistinct, incomplete image, both of night itself and of what it contains. Thus also with *oscurità* [darkness], *profondo* [deep]).

Leopardi's reasoning is perfectly exemplified by his poems, which lend it the authority of what is proven by facts. Leafing again through the *Zibaldone* in search of other examples of this passion of his, I come across one entry longer than usual, a list of situations propitious to the "indefinite" state of mind:

> la luce del sole o della luna, veduta in luogo dov'essi non si vedano e non si scopra la sorgente della luce; un luogo solamente in parte illuminato da essa luce; il riflesso di detta luce, e i vari effetti materiali che ne derivano; il penetrare di detta luce in luoghi dov'ella divenga incerta e impedita, e non bene si distingua, come attraverso un canneto, in una selva, per li balconi socchiusi ec. ec.; la detta luce veduta in luogo, oggetto ec. dov'ella non entri e non percota dirittamente, ma vi sia ribattuta e diffusa da qualche altro luogo od oggetto ec. dov'ella venga a battere; in un andito veduto al di dentro o al di fuori, e in una loggia parimente ec. quei luoghi dove la luce si confonde ec. ec. colle ombre, come sotto un portico, in una loggia elevata e pensile, fra le rupi e i burroni, in una valle, sui colli veduti

dalla parte dell'ombra, in modo che ne sieno indorate le cime; il riflesso che produce, per esempio, un vetro colorato su quegli oggetti su cui si riflettono i raggi che passano per detto vetro; tutti quegli oggetti insomma che per diverse materiali e menome circostanze giungono alla nostra vista, *udito* ec. in modo incerto, mal distinto, imperfetto, incompleto, o fuor dell'ordinario ec.

the light of the sun or the moon, seen in a place from which they are invisible and one cannot discern the source of the light; a place only partly illuminated by such light; the reflection of such light, and the various material effects derived from it; the penetration of such light into places where it becomes uncertain and obstructed, and is not easily made out, as through a cane brake, in a wood, through half-closed shutters, etc., etc.; the same light in a place, object, etc., where it does not enter and strike directly, reflected and diffused by some other place or object, etc., where it does strike; in a passageway seen from inside or outside, and similarly in a loggia, etc., places where the light mingles, etc., etc., with the shadows, as under a portico, in a high, overhanging loggia, among rocks and gullies, in a valley, on hills seen from the shady side so that their crests are gilded; the reflection produced, for example, by a colored pane of glass on those objects on which the rays passing through that glass are reflected; all those objects, in a word, that by means of various materials and minimal circumstances come to our sight, *hearing,* etc., in a way that is uncertain, indistinct, imperfect, incomplete, or out of the ordinary.

So this is what Leopardi asks of us, that we may savor the beauty of the vague and indefinite! What he requires is a highly exact and meticulous attention to the composition of each image, to the minute definition of details, to the choice of objects, to the lighting and the atmosphere, all in order to attain the desired degree of vagueness. Therefore Leopardi, whom I had chosen as the ideal opponent of my argument in favor of exactitude, turns out to be a decisive witness in its favor . . . . . The poet of vagueness can only be the poet of exactitude, who is able to grasp the subtlest sensations with eyes and ears and quick, unerring hands. It is worthwhile to read this note in the *Zibaldone* right to the end, since the search for the indefinite becomes the observation of all that is multiple, teeming, composed of countless particles.

Per lo contrario la vista del sole o della luna in una campagna vasta ed aprica, e in un cielo aperto ec. è piacevole per la vastità della sensazione. Ed è pur piacevole per la ragione assegnata di sopra, la vista di un cielo diversamente sparso di nuvoletti, dove la luce del sole o della luna produca effetti *variati,* e indistinti, e non ordinari ec. È piacevolissima e sentimentalissima la stessa luce veduta nelle città, dov'ella è frastagliata dalle ombre, dove lo scuro contrasta in molti luoghi col chiaro, dove la luce in molte parti degrada appoco appoco, come sui tetti, dove alcuni luoghi riposti nascondono la vista dell'astro luminoso ec. ec. A questo piacere contribuisce la varietà, l'incertezza, il non veder tutto, e il potersi perciò spaziare coll'immaginazionè, riguardo a ciò che non si vede. Similmente dico dei simili effetti, che producono gli alberi, i filari, i colli, i pergolati, i casolari, i pagliai, le ineguaglianze del suolo ec. nelle campagne. Per lo contrario una vasta e tutta uguale pianura, dove la luce si spazi e diffonda senza diversità, nè ostacolo; dove l'occhio si perda ec. è pure piacevolissima, per l'idea indefinita in estensione, che deriva da tal veduta. Così un cielo senza nuvolo. Nel qual proposito osservo che il piacere della varietà e dell'incertezza prevale a quello dell'apparente infinità, e dell'immensa uniformità. E quindi un cielo variamente sparso di nuvoletti, è forse più piacevole di un cielo affatto puro; e la vista del cielo è forse meno piacevole di quella della terra, e delle campagne ec. perchè meno varia (ed anche meno simile a noi, meno propria di noi, meno appartenente alle cose nostre ec.). Infatti, ponetevi supino in modo che voi non vediate se non il cielo, separato dalla terra, voi proverete una sensazione molto meno piacevole che considerando una campagna, o considerando il cielo nella sua corrispondenza e relazione colla terra, ed unitamente ad essa in un medesimo punto di vista.

È piacevolissima ancora, per le sopraddette cagioni, la vista di una moltitudine innumerabile, come delle stelle, o di persone ec. un moto moltiplice, incerto, confuso, irregolare, disordinato, un ondeggiamento vago ec., che l'animo non possa determinare, nè concepire definitamente e distintamente ec., come quello di una folla, o di un gran numero di formiche o del mare agitato ec. Similmente una moltitudine di suoni irregolarmente mescolati, e non distinguibili l'uno dall'altro ec. ec. ec. (20 Settembre 1821).*

By contrast, the sight of the sun or moon in a vast, airy landscape, and in a clear sky, etc., is pleasing for the vastness of the sensation. And also pleasing, for the reason mentioned above, is the sight of the sky dotted with little clouds, in which the light of the sun or the moon produces *varied* effects, indistinct, out of the ordinary, etc. Most pleasing and full of feeling is the light seen in cities, where

* *Zibaldone di pensieri*, 2 vols., ed. Francesco Flora (Milan: Mondadori, 1937), I.1145, 1150, 1123–25.

it is slashed by shadows, where darkness contrasts in many places with light, where in many parts the light little by little grows less, as on rooftops, where a few secluded places hide the luminous body from our sight, etc., etc. Contributing to this pleasure is the variety, the uncertainty, the not-seeing-everything, and therefore being able to walk abroad using the imagination in regard to what one does not see. I say similar things of similar effects produced by trees, rows of vines, hills, pergolas, outlying houses, hay-stacks, wrinkles in the soil, etc., of the landscape. On the contrary, a vast level plain, where the light sweeps and spreads without variety or obstacle, where the eye loses itself, etc., is also highly pleasurable, for the idea of infinite extension that results from such a sight. The same is true of a cloudless sky. In this regard I observe that the pleasure of variety and uncertainty is greater than that of apparent infinity and immense uniformity. And therefore a sky dotted with small clouds is perhaps more pleasurable than a totally clear sky; and to look at the sky is perhaps less pleasurable than to look at the earth and the landscape, etc., because it is less varied (and also less like us, less of our own, belonging less to things that are ours, etc.). In fact, if you lie down on your back so that you see nothing but the sky, separated from the earth, you will have a far less pleasing feeling than if you look at a landscape, or look at the sky in proportion and relation to the earth, integrating them from the same point of view.

Highly pleasing also, for the above-mentioned reasons, is the sight of an innumerable multitude, as of stars, people, etc., a multiple motion, uncertain, confused, irregular, dis-ordered, a vague rising and falling, etc., which the mind cannot conceive definitely or distinctly, etc., like that of a crowd, or a swarm of ants, or a rough sea, etc. Similarly a multitude of sounds, irregularly mingled together, not to be distinguished one from another.

Here we touch on one of the nerve centers of Leopardi's poetics, as embodied in his most famous and beautiful lyric, "L'infinito." Protected by a hedge, on the far side of which he sees only the sky, the poet imagines infinite space and feels pleasure and fear together. The poem dates from 1819. The notes I read from the *Zibaldone* date from two years later and show that Leopardi went on thinking about the problem aroused by the composition of "L'infinito." In his reflections, two terms are constantly compared: the "indefinite" and the "infinite." For Leopardi, unhappy hedonist that he was, what is unknown is always more attractive than what is known; hope and imagination are the only consolations for the disappointments and sorrows of experience. Man therefore projects his desire into infinity and feels pleasure only when he is able to imagine that this pleasure has no end. But since the human mind cannot conceive the infinite, and in fact falls back aghast at the very idea of it, it has to make do with what is indefinite, with sensations as they mingle together and create an impression of infinite space, illusory but pleasurable all the same: "E il naufragar m'è dolce in questo mare" (And sweet to me is foundering in this sea). It is not only in the famous ending of "L'infinito" that gentleness prevails over fear, for what the lines communicate by the music of the words is, throughout, a sense of gentleness, even when these words express anguish.

I realize that I am interpreting Leopardi purely in terms of sensations, as if I accepted the image he wants to give of himself as a disciple of eighteenth-century Sensism. In fact the problem Leopardi is facing is speculative and metaphysical, a problem in the history of philosophy from Parmenides to Descartes and Kant: the relationship between the idea of infinity as absolute space and absolute time, and our empirical knowledge of space and time. Leopardi therefore starts with the rigorous abstraction of a mathematical notion of space and time, and compares this to the vague, undefined flux of sensations.

So, too, exactitude and lack of definition are the poles between which the philosophical and ironic thoughts of the character Ulrich oscillate in the endless (and indeed unfinished) novel by Robert Musil, *Der Mann ohne Eigenschaften* (The Man without Qualities):

> Ist nun das beobachtete Element die Exaktheit selbst, hebt man es heraus und lässt es sich entwickeln, betrachtet man es als Denkgewohnheit und Lebenshaltung und lässt es seine beispielgebende Kraft auf alles auswirken, was mit ihm in Berührung kommt, so wird man zu einem Menschen geführt, in dem eine paradoxe Verbindung von Genauigkeit und Unbestimmtheit stattfindet. Er besitzt jene unbestechliche gewollte Kaltblütigkeit, die das Temperament der Exaktheit darstellt; über diese Eigenschaft hinaus ist aber alles andere unbestimmt. (I, part 2, chap. 61; Rowolt edition, 1978, I.246–247)

> If now the element under observation is exactitude itself, if one isolates it and allows it to develop, if one regards it as an intellectual habit and a way of living and lets it exert its exemplary influence on everything that comes into contact with it, the logical conclusion is a human being with the paradoxical combination of precision and indefiniteness. He possesses an incorruptible, deliberate cold-

bloodedness, the temperament that goes with exactitude; but apart from and beyond this quality, all is indefinite.

The point at which Musil comes closest to a possible solution is when he mentions the fact that mathematical problems do not admit of a general solution, but that particular solutions, taken all together, can lead to a general solution (chap. 83). He thinks that this method might be applied to human life. Many years later another writer, Roland Barthes, in whose mind the demon of exactitude lived side by side with the demon of sensitivity, asked himself if it would not be possible to conceive of a science of the unique and unrepeatable: "Pourquoi n'y aurait-il pas, en quelque sorte, une science nouvelle par objet? Une *Mathesis singularis* (et non plus *universalis*)?"[*La chambre claire,* 1980, p. 21] (Why couldn't there be, in some way, a new science for every object? A *mathesis singularis*, and no longer *universalis*?).

If Musil's Ulrich soon resigns himself to the defeats that the passion for exactitude is bound to suffer, Paul Valéry's Monsieur Teste, another great intellectual personage of this century, has no doubts about the fact that the human spirit can fulfill itself in the most exact and rigorous way. And if Leopardi, poet of life's sadness, shows the highest degree of exactitude in describing indefinite sensations that give pleasure, Valéry, poet of impassive rigor of mind, shows the highest degree of exactitude in putting his Monsieur Teste face to face with pain, and making him combat physical suffering by an exercise in abstract geometry.

"J'ai," dit-il . . . "pas grand'chose. J'ai . . . un dixième de seconde qui se montre . . . Attendez . . . Il y a des instants où mon corps s'illumine . . . C'est très curieux. J'y vois tout à coup en moi . . . je distingue les profondeurs des couches de ma chair; et je sens des zones de douleur, des anneaux, des pôles, des aigrettes de douleur. Voyez-vous ces figures vives? cette géométrie de ma souffrance? Il y a de ces éclairs qui ressemblent tout à fait à des idées. Ils font comprendre—d'ici, jusque-là ... Et pourtant ils me laissent *incertain*. Incertain n'est pas le mot ... Quand *cela* va venir, je trouve en moi quelque chose de confus ou de diffus. Il se fait dans mon être des endroits ... brumeux, il y a des étendues qui font leur apparition. Alors, je prends dans ma mémoire une question, un problème quelconque ... Je m'y enfonce. Je compte des grains de sable ... et, tant que je les vois ... — Ma douleur grossissante me force à l'observer. J'y pense!—Je n'attends que mon cri ... et dès que je l'ai entendu—l'*objet,* le terrible *objet,* devenant plus petit, et encore plus petit, se dérobe à ma vue intérieure." (Gallimard edition, 1946, pp. 32–33)

"It is nothing ... much," he said. "Nothing but ... a tenth of a second appearing ... Wait ... At certain moments my body is illuminated ... It is very curious. Suddenly I see into myself ... I can make out the depths of the layers of my flesh; and I feel zones of pain ... rings, poles, plumes of pain. Do you see these living forms, this geometry of my suffering? Some of these flashes are exactly like ideas. They make me understand—from here, to there ... And yet they leave me *uncertain*. Uncertain is not the word ... When *it* is about to appear, I find in myself something confused or diffused. Areas that are ... hazy occur inside me, wide spaces come into view. Then I choose a question from my memory, any problem at all ... I plunge into it. I count grains of sand ... and as long as I can see them ... But increasing pain forces me to observe it. I think about it! I only await my cry ... and as soon as I have heard it—the *object,* the terrible *object,* getting smaller, and still smaller, vanishes from my inner sight."

In our century Paul Valéry is the one who has best defined poetry as a straining toward exactitude. I am speaking chiefly of his work as a critic and essayist, in which the poetics of exactitude may be traced in a straight line through Mallarmé to Baudelaire and from Baudelaire to Edgar Allan Poe.

In Poe—the Poe of Baudelaire and Mallarmé—Valéry sees "le démon de la lucidité, le génie de l'analyse, et l'inventeur des combinaisons les plus neuves et les plus séduisantes de la logique avec l'imagination, de la mysticité avec le calcul, le psychologue de l'exception, l'ingénieur littéraire qui approfondit et utilise toutes les ressources de l'art" (the demon of lucidity, the genius of analysis, and the inventor of the newest, most seductive combinations of logic and imagination, of mysticism and calculation; the psychologist of the exceptional; the literary engineer who studied and utilized all the resources of art). Valéry writes this in his essay "Situation de Baudelaire," which for me has the value of a poetic manifesto, together with another essay of his on Poe and cosmogony, in which he deals with *Eureka*.

In the essay on Poe's *Eureka*, Valéry questions himself on cosmogony as a literary genre rather than as scientific speculation and achieves a brilliant refutation of the idea of "universe," which is also a reaffirmation of the mythic force that every image of "universe" carries with it. Here too, as in Leopardi, we find both attraction and repulsion with regard to the infinite. And here too we find cosmological conjectures as a literary genre, such as Leopardi amused himself with in certain "apocryphal" prose pieces: "Frammento apocrifo di Stratone da Lampsaco" (Apocryphal Fragment of Strato of Lampsacus), on the beginning and particularly the end of the terrestrial globe, which flattens and empties out like the rings of Saturn and is dispersed until it burns up in the sun; or his translation of an apocryphal Talmudic text, "Cantico del gallo silvestre" (Song of the Great Wild Rooster), where the entire universe is extinguished and disappears: "un silenzio nudo, e una quiete altissima, empieranno lo spazio immenso. Così questo arcano mirabile e spaventoso dell'esistenza universale, innanzi di essere dichiarato nè inteso, si dileguerà e perderassi" (a naked silence and a most profound quiet will fill the immensity of space. So this marvelous and frightening mystery of universal existence, before being declared or understood, will fade away and be lost). Here we see that what is terrifying and inconceivable is not the infinite void, but existence.

This talk is refusing to be led in the direction I set myself. I began by speaking of exactitude, not of the infinite and the cosmos. I wanted to tell you of my fondness for geometrical forms, for symmetries, for numerical series, for all that is combinatory, for numerical proportions; I wanted to explain the things I had written in terms of my fidelity to the idea of limits, of measure . . . . . But perhaps it is precisely this idea of forms that evokes the idea of the endless: the sequence of whole numbers, Euclid's straight lines . . . . . Rather than speak to you of what I have written, perhaps it would be more interesting to tell you about the problems that I have *not* yet resolved, that I don't know how to resolve, and what these will cause me to write: Sometimes I try to concentrate on the story I would like to write, and I realize that what interests me is something else entirely or, rather, not anything precise but everything that does not fit in with what I ought to write—the relationship between a given argument and all its possible variants and alternatives, everything that can happen in time and space. This is a devouring and destructive obsession, which is enough to render writing impossible. In order to combat it, I try to limit the field of what I have to say, divide it into still more limited fields, then subdivide these again, and so on and on. Then another kind of vertigo seizes me, that of the detail of the detail of the detail, and I am drawn into the infinitesimal, the infinitely small, just as I was previously lost in the infinitely vast.

"Le bon Dieu est dans le détail." This statement of Flaubert's I would explain in the light of the philosophy of Giordano Bruno, that great visionary cosmologist, who sees the universe as infinite and composed of innumerable worlds but who cannot call it "totally infinite" because each of these worlds is finite. God, on the other hand, *is* totally infinite: "tutto lui è in tutto il mondo, ed in ciascuna sua parte infinitamente e totalmente" (the whole of him is in the whole world, and in each of his parts infinitely and totally).

Among the Italian books in the last few years which I have most often read, reread, and thought about is Paolo Zellini's *Breve storia dell' infinito* (Short History of the Infinite, 1980). It opens with Borges' famous invective against the infinite from "Avatares de la tortuga" (Avatars of the Tortoise)—it is the one concept that corrupts and confuses all others—and then goes on to review all arguments on the subject, with the result that it dissolves and reverses the extension of the infinite into the density of the infinitesimal.

I think that this bond between the formal choices of literary composition and the need for a cosmological model (or else for a general mythological framework) is present even in those authors who do not explicitly declare it. This taste for geometrical composition, of which we could trace a history in world literature starting with Mallarmé, is based on the contrast of order and disorder fundamental to contemporary science. The universe disintegrates into a cloud of heat, it falls inevitably into a vortex of entropy, but within this irreversible process there may be areas of order, portions of the existent that tend toward a form, privileged points in which we seem to discern a design or perspective. A work of literature is one of these minimal portions in which the existent crystallizes into a form, acquires a meaning—not fixed, not definitive, not hardened into a mineral immobility, but alive as an organism. Poetry is the great enemy of chance, in spite of also being a daughter of chance and knowing that, in the last resort, chance will win the battle. "Un coup de dés n'abolira jamais le hasard" (One throw of the dice will never annul chance).

It is in this context that we should view the reevaluation of logical, geometrical, and metaphysical procedures that prevailed in the figurative arts during the first decades of this century and thereafter in literature. The emblem of the crystal might be used to distinguish a whole constellation of poets and writers, very different from one another, such as Paul Valéry in France, Wallace Stevens in the United States, Gottfried Benn in Germany, Fernando Pessoa in Portugal, Ramon Gómez de la Serna in Spain, Massimo Bontempelli in Italy, and Jorge Luis Borges in Argentina.

The crystal, with its precise faceting and its ability to refract light, is the model of perfection that I have always cherished as an emblem, and this predilection has become even more meaningful since we have learned that certain properties of the birth and growth of crystals resemble those of the most rudimentary biological creatures, forming a kind of bridge between the mineral world and living matter.

Among the scientific books into which I poke my nose in search of stimulus for the imagination, I recently happened to read that the models for the process of formation of living beings "are best visualized by the *crystal* on one side (invariance of specific structures) and the *flame* on the other (constancy of external forms in spite of relentless internal agitation)." I am quoting from Massimo Piattelli-Palmarini's introduction to the volume devoted to the debate between Jean Piaget and Noam Chomsky in

1975 at the Centre Royaumont (*Language and Learning,* 1980, p. 6). The contrasting images of flame and crystal are used to make visible the alternatives offered to biology, and from this pass on to theories of language and the ability to learn. For the moment I will leave aside the implications for the philosophy of science embodied in the positions stated by Piaget, who is for the principle of "order out of noise"—the flame—and Chomsky, who is for the "self-organizing system," the crystal.

What interests me here is the juxtaposition of these two symbols, as in one of those sixteenth-century emblems I mentioned in my last lecture. Crystal and flame: two forms of perfect beauty that we cannot tear our eyes away from, two modes of growth in time, of expenditure of the matter surrounding them, two moral symbols, two absolutes, two categories for classifying facts and ideas, styles and feelings. A short while ago I suggested a "Party of the Crystal" in twentieth-century literature, and I think one could draw up a similar list for a "Party of the Flame." I have always considered myself a partisan of the crystal, but the passage just quoted teaches me not to forget the value of the flame as a way of being, as a mode of existence. In the same way, I would like those who think of themselves as disciples of the flame not to lose sight of the tranquil, arduous lesson of the crystal.

A more complex symbol, which has given me greater possibilities of expressing the tension between geometric rationality and the entanglements of human lives, is that of the city. The book in which I think I managed to say most remains *Invisible Cities,* because I was able to concentrate all my reflections, experiments, and conjectures on a single symbol; and also because I built up a many-faceted structure in which each brief text is close to the others in a series that does not imply logical sequence or a hierarchy, but a network in which one can follow multiple routes and draw multiple, ramified conclusions.

In my *Invisible Cities* every concept and value turns out to be double—even exactitude. At a certain point Kublai Khan personifies the intellectual tendency toward rationalization, geometry, and algebra, reducing knowledge of his empire to the combinatoria of pieces on a chessboard. The cities that Marco Polo describes to him with a wealth of detail Kublai represents with various arrangements of castles, bishops, knights, kings, queens, and pawns on black and white squares. The final conclusion to which this operation leads him is that the object of his conquest is nothing other than the block of wood on which each piece rests: an emblem of nothingness. But just at this moment comes a *coup de scène,* for Marco Polo requests Kublai to look more closely at what he sees as nothingness:

Il Gran Kan cercava d'immedesimarsi nel gioco: ma adesso era il perché del gioco a sfuggirgli. Il fine d'ogni partita è una vincita o una perdita: ma di cosa? Qual era la vera posta? Allo scacco matto, sotto il piede del re sbalzato via dalla mano del vincitore, resta il nulla: un quadrato nero o bianco. A forza di scorporare le sue conquiste per ridurle all'essenza, Kublai era arrivato all'operazione estrema: la conquista definitiva, di cui i multiformi tesori dell'impero non erano che involucri illusori, si riduceva a un tassello di legno piallato.

Allora Marco Polo parlò:—La tua scacchiera, sire, è un intarsio di due legni: ebano e acero. Il tassello sul quale si fissa il tuo sguardo illuminato fu tagliato in uno strato del tronco che crebbe in un anno di siccità: vedi come si dispongono le fibre? Qui si scorge un nodo appena accennato: una gemma tentò di spuntare in un giorno di primavera precoce, ma la brina della notte l'obbligò a desistere—. Il Gran Kan non s'era fin'allora reso conto che lo straniero sapesse esprimersi fluentemente nella sua lingua, ma non era questo a stupirlo.—Ecco un poro più grosso: forse è stato il nido d'una larva; non d'un tarlo, perché appena nato avrebbe continuato a scavare, ma d'un bruco che rosicchiò le foglie e fu la causa per cui l'albero fu scelto per essere abbattuto . . . Questo margine fu inciso dall'ebanista con la sgorbia perché aderisse al quadrato vicino, piú sporgente . . .

La quantità di cose che si potevano leggere in un pezzetto di legno liscio e vuoto sommergeva Kublai; già Polo era venuto a parlare dei boschi d'ebano, delle zattere di tronchi che discendono i fiumi, degli approdi, delle donne alle finestre . . .

The Great Khan tried to concentrate on the game: but now it was the game's reason that eluded him. The end of every game is a gain or a loss: but of what? What were the real stakes? At checkmate, beneath the foot of the king, knocked aside by the winner's hand, nothingness remains: a black square, or a white one. By disembodying his conquests to reduce them to the essential, Kublai had arrived at the extreme operation: the definitive conquest, of which the empire's multiform treasures were only illusory envelopes; it was reduced to a square of planed wood.

Then Marco Polo spoke: "Your chessboard, sire, is inlaid with two woods: ebony and maple. The square on which your enlightened gaze is fixed was cut from the ring of a trunk that grew in a year of drought: you see how its fibers are arranged? Here a barely hinted knot can be made out: a bud tried to burgeon on a premature spring day, but the night's frost forced it to desist."

Until then the Great Khan had not realized that the

foreigner knew how to express himself fluently in his language, but it was not this fluency that amazed him.

"Here is a thicker pore: perhaps it was a larvum's nest; not a woodworm, because, once born, it would have begun to dig, but a caterpillar that gnawed the leaves and was the cause of the tree's being chosen for chopping down . . . This edge was scored by the wood carver with his gouge so that it would adhere to the next square, more protruding. . . ."

The quantity of things that could be read in a little piece of smooth and empty wood overwhelmed Kublai; Polo was already talking about ebony forests, about rafts laden with logs that come down the rivers, of docks, of women at the windows . . .*

From the moment I wrote that page it became clear to me that my search for exactitude was branching out in two directions: on the one side, the reduction of secondary events to abstract patterns according to which one can carry out operations and demonstrate theorems; and on the other, the effort made by words to present the tangible aspect of things as precisely as possible.

The fact is, my writing has always found itself facing two divergent paths that correspond to two different types of knowledge. One path goes into the mental space of bodiless rationality, where one may trace lines that converge, projections, abstract forms, vectors of force. The other path goes through a space crammed with objects and attempts to create a verbal equivalent of that space by filling the page with words, involving a most careful, painstaking effort to adapt what is written to what is not written, to the sum of what is sayable and not sayable. These are two different drives toward exactitude that will never attain com-

---

*Invisible Cities, translated by William Weaver (New York: Harcourt Brace Jovanovich, 1974), pp. 131–132.

plete fulfillment, one because "natural" languages always say something *more* than formalized languages can—natural languages always involve a certain amount of noise that impinges upon the essentiality of the information—and the other because, in representing the density and continuity of the world around us, language is revealed as defective and fragmentary, always saying something *less* with respect to the sum of what can be experienced.

I continually switch back and forth between these two paths, and when I feel I have fully explored the possibilities of one, I rush across to the other, and vice versa. Thus in the last few years I have alternated my exercises in the structure of the story with other exercises in description, today a very neglected art. Like a schoolboy whose homework is to "Describe a giraffe" or "Describe the starry sky," I applied myself to filling a notebook with such exercises and made a book out of the material. This is *Mr. Palomar,* which was recently published in English translation (1985). It is a kind of diary dealing with minimal problems of knowledge, ways of establishing relationships with the world, and gratifications and frustrations in the use of both silence and words.

In my quests of this sort I have always borne in mind the practice of poets. I think of William Carlos Williams, who describes the leaves of the cyclamen so minutely that we can visualize the flower poised above the leaves he has drawn for us, thereby giving the poem the delicacy of the plant. I think of Marianne Moore who, in depicting her scaly anteater and her nautilus and all the other animals in her bestiary, blends information from zoology books with symbolic and allegorical meanings that make each of her poems a moral fable. And I think also of Eugenio Montale, who may be said to sum up the achievement of both in his poem, "L'anguilla." This is a poem consisting of a single very long sentence in the shape of an eel, following the entire life of the eel, and making the eel into a moral symbol.

But above all I think of Francis Ponge because, with his little prose poems, he created a genre unique in contemporary literature: that schoolboy's "exercise book" in which he has to start by practicing arranging his words as an extension of the appearances of the world, and going through a series of tryouts, *brouillons,* approximations. Ponge for me is a peerless master because the brief texts of *Le parti pris des choses* (The Purpose of Things) and his other books on similar lines, speaking of a shrimp or a pebble or a cake of soap, give us the best example of a battle to force language to become the language of *things,* starting from things and returning to us changed, with all the humanity that we have invested in things. Ponge's declared intention was, by means of his brief texts and their elaborate variants, to compose a new *De Rerum Natura.* I believe that he may be the Lucretius of our time, reconstructing the physical nature of the world by means of the impalpable, powder-fine dust of words.

It seems to me that Ponge's achievement is on the same level as Mallarmé's, though in a divergent and complementary direction. In Mallarmé the word attains the acme of exactitude by reaching the last degree of abstraction and by showing nothingness to be the ultimate substance of the world. In Ponge the world takes the form of the most humble, secondary, and asymmetrical things, and the word is what serves to make us aware of the infinite variety of these irregular, minutely complicated forms.

There are those who hold that the word is the way of attaining the substance of the world, the final, unique, and absolute substance. Rather than representing this substance, the word identifies itself with it (so that it is wrong to call the word merely a means to an end): there is the word that knows only itself, and no other knowledge of the world is possible. There are others who regard the use of the word as an unceasing pursuit of things, an approach not to their substance but to their infinite variety, touching on their inexhaustibly multiform surface. As Hoffmannsthal said: "Depth is hidden. Where? On the surface." And Wittgenstein went even further than this: "For what is hidden . . . is of no interest to us."

I would not be so drastic. I think we are always searching for something hidden or merely potential or hypothetical, following its traces whenever they appear on the surface. I think our basic mental processes have come down to us through every period of history, ever since the times of our Paleolithic forefathers, who were hunters and gatherers. The word connects the visible trace with the invisible thing, the absent thing, the thing that is desired or feared, like a frail emergency bridge flung over an abyss.

For this reason, the proper use of language, for me personally, is one that enables us to approach things (present or absent) with discretion, attention, and caution, with respect for what things (present or absent) communicate without words.

Leonardo da Vinci offers a significant example of the battle with language to capture something that evaded his powers of expression. Leonardo's codices comprise an extraordinary documentation of struggle with language, a gnarled, spiky language, from which he seeks richer, more subtle, and more precise expression. The various phases in the treatment of an idea—like those of Francis Ponge, who ends by publishing them in sequence because the real work consists not in its definitive form, but in the series of approximations made to attain it—are, for Leonardo as writer, the proof of the effort he invested in writing as an instrument of knowledge; and also of the fact that, in the case of all the books he thought of writing, he was more interested in the process of inquiry than in the completion of a text for publication. From time to time, even the subjects are similar to Ponge's as in the series of short fables that Leonardo wrote about objects or animals.

Let us take the fable about fire, for example. Leonardo gives us a rapid summary: the fire, offended because the water in the pan is above him, although he is the "higher" element, shoots his flames up and up until the water boils, overflows, and puts him out. Leonardo then elaborates this in three successive drafts, all of them incomplete, written in three parallel columns. Each time he adds some details, describing how, from a little piece of charcoal, a flame bursts through the gaps in the wood, crackling and swelling. But he soon breaks off, as if becoming aware that there is no limit to the minuteness of detail with which one can tell even the simplest story. Even a tale of wood catching fire in the kitchen fireplace can grow from within until it becomes infinite.

Leonardo, "omo sanza lettere" (an unlettered man), as he described himself, had a difficult relationship with the written word. His knowledge was without equal in all the world, but his ignorance of Latin and grammar prevented him from communicating in writing with the learned men of his time. Certainly he thought he could set down much of his science more clearly in drawings than in words. "O scrittore, con quali lettere scriverai tu con tal perfezione la intera figurazione qual fa qui il disegno?" (O writer, with what letters can you convey the entire figuration with such perfection as drawing gives us here?), he wrote in his notebooks on anatomy. And not just in science but also in philosophy, he was confident he could communicate better by means of painting and drawing. Still he also felt an incessant need to write, to use writing to investigate the world in all its polymorphous manifestations and secrets, and also to give shape to his fantasies, emotions, and rancors—as when he inveighs against men of letters, who were able only to repeat what they had read in the books of others, unlike those who were among the "inventori e interpreti tra la natura e li omini" (inventors and interpreters between nature and men). He therefore wrote more and more. With the passing of the years, he gave up painting and expressed himself through writing and drawing, as if following the thread of a single discourse in drawings and in words, filling his notebooks with his left-handed mirror writing.

On folio 265 of the Codex Atlanticus, Leonardo begins to jot down evidence to prove a theory of the growth of the earth. After giving examples of buried cities swallowed up by the soil, he goes on to the marine fossils found in the mountains and in particular to certain bones that he supposes must have belonged to an antediluvian sea monster. At this moment his imagination must have been caught by a vision of the immense animal as it was swimming among the waves. At any rate, he turns the page upside down and tries to capture the image of the animal, three times attempting a sentence that will convey all the wonder of that evocation.

O quante volte fusti tu veduto in fra l'onde del gonfiato e grande oceano, col setoluto e nero dosso, a guisa di montagna e con grave e superbo andamento!

O how many times were you seen among the waves of the great swollen ocean, with your black and bristly back, looming like a mountain, and with grave and stately bearing!

Then he tries to give more movement to the monster's progress by introducing the verb *volteggiare* (to whirl).

E spesse volte eri veduto in fra l'onde del gonfiato e grande oceano, e col superbo e grave moto gir volteggiando in fra le marine acque. E con setoluto e nero dosso, a guisa di montagna, quelle vincere e sopraffare!

And many times were you seen among the waves of the great swollen ocean, and with stately and grave bearing go swirling in the sea waters. And with your black and bristly back, looming like a mountain, defeating and overwhelming them!

But the word *volteggiare* seems to him to have lessened the impression of grandeur and majesty that he wants to evoke. So he chooses the verb *solcare* (to furrow) and alters the whole construction of the passage, giving it compactness and rhythm with sure literary judgment:

O quante volte fusti tu veduto in fra l'onde del gonfiato e grande oceano, a guisa di montagna quelle vincere e sopraffare, e col setoluto e nero dosso solcare le marine acque, e con superbo e grave andamento!

O how many times were you seen among the waves of the great swollen ocean, looming like a mountain, defeating and overwhelming them, and with your black and bristly back furrowing the sea waters, and with stately and grave bearing!

His pursuit of the apparition, which is presented almost as a symbol of the solemn force of nature, gives us an inkling of how Leonardo's imagination worked. I leave you this image at the very end of my talk so that you may carry it in your memories as long as possible, in all its transparency and its mystery.

4

VISIBILITY

There is a line in Dante (*Purgatorio* XVII.25) that reads: "Poi piovve dentro a l'alta fantasia" (Then rained down into the high fantasy . . .). I will start out this evening with an assertion: fantasy is a place where it rains.

Let us look at the context in which we find this line of the *Purgatorio*. We are in the circle of the Wrathful, and Dante is meditating on images that form directly in his mind, depicting classical and biblical examples of wrath chastised. He realizes that these images rain down from the heavens—that is, God sends them to him.

In the various circles of Purgatory, besides the details of the landscape and the vault of the heavens, and in addition to his encounters with the souls of repentant sinners and with supernatural beings, Dante is presented with scenes that act as quotations or representations of examples of sins and virtues, at first as bas-reliefs that appear to move and to speak, then as visions projected before his eyes, then as voices reaching his ear, and finally as purely mental images. In a word, these visions turn progressively more inward, as if Dante realized that it is useless at every circle to invent a new form of metarepresentation, and that it is better to place the visions directly in the mind without making them pass through the senses.

But before this it is necessary to define what the imagination is, and this Dante does in two terzinas (XVII.13–18):

O imaginativa che ne rube
talvolta sì di fuor, ch'om non s'accorge
perché dintorno suonin mille tube,
   chi move te, se 'l senso non ti porge?
Moveti lume che nel ciel s'informa
per sé o per voler che giù lo scorge.

It goes without saying that we are here concerned with "high fantasy": that is, with the loftier part of the imagination as distinct from the corporeal imagination, such as is revealed in the chaos of dreams. With this point in mind, let us try to follow Dante's reasoning, which faithfully reproduces that of the philosophy of his time. I will paraphrase: O imagination, you who have the power to impose yourself on our faculties and our wills, stealing us away from the outer world and carrying us off into an inner one, so that even if a thousand trumpets were to sound we would not hear them, what is the source of the visual messages that you receive, if they are not formed from sensations deposited in the memory? "Moveti lume che nel ciel s'informa" (You are moved by a light that is formed in heaven): according to Dante—and also Thomas Aquinas—there is a kind of luminous source in the skies that transmits ideal images, which are formed either according to the intrinsic logic of the imaginary world ("per sé") or according to the will of God: "o per voler che giù lo scorge" (or by a will that guides it downward).

Dante speaks of the visions presented to him (that is, to Dante the actor in the poem) almost as if they were film projections or television images seen on a screen that is quite separate from the objective reality of his journey beyond the earth. But for Dante the poet as well, the entire journey of Dante the actor is of the same nature as these visions. The poet has to imagine visually both what his actor sees and what he thinks he sees, what he dreams, what he remembers, what he sees represented, or what is told to him, just as he has to imagine the visual content of the metaphors he uses to facilitate this process of visual evocation. What Dante is attempting to define, therefore, is the role of the imagination in the *Commedia,* in particular the visual part of his fantasy, which precedes or is simultaneous with verbal imagination.

We may distinguish between two types of imaginative process: the one that starts with the word and arrives at the visual image, and the one that starts with the visual image and arrives at its verbal expression. The first process is the one that normally occurs when we read. For example, we read a scene in a novel or the report of some event in a newspaper and, according to the greater or lesser effectiveness of the text, we are brought to witness the scene as if it were taking place before our eyes, or at least to witness certain fragments or details of the scene that are singled out.

In the cinema the image we see on the screen has also passed through the stage of a written text, has then been "visualized" in the mind of the director, then physically reconstructed on the set, and finally fixed in the frames of the film itself. A film is therefore the outcome of a succession of phases, both material and otherwise, in the course of which the images acquire form. During this process, the "mental cinema" of the imagination has a function no less important than that of the actual creation of the sequences as they will be recorded by the camera and then put together on the moviola. This mental cinema is always at work in each one of us, and it always has been, even before the invention of the cinema. Nor does it ever stop projecting images before our mind's eye.

It is significant that great importance is given to the visual imagination in Ignatius of Loyola's *Ejercicios espirituales* (Spiritual

Exercises). At the beginning of his manual, Loyola prescribes the
"composición viendo el lugar" (visual composition of the place)
in terms that might be instructions for the mise-en-scène of a
theatrical performance: "en la contemplación o meditación visible, así como contemplar a Christo nuestro Señor, el qual es
visible, la composición será ver con la vista de la imaginación el
lugar corpóreo, donde se halla la cosa que quiero contemplar.
Digo el lugar corpóreo, así como un templo o monte, donde se
halla Jesu Christo o Nuestra Señora," (in visual contemplation or
meditation, especially in the contemplation of Christ our Lord
insofar as he is visible, this composition will consist in seeing
from the view of the imagination the physical place where the
thing I wish to contemplate is to be found. I say the physical
place, as for example a temple or a hill where Jesus Christ or
Our Lady is). Loyola quickly hastens to make it clear that the
contemplation of our own sins must not be visual, or else—if I
have understood rightly—we must make use of visual imagination of a metaphorical sort (the soul imprisoned in the corrup-
tible body).

Further on, in the first day of the second week, the spiritual
exercise opens with a vast visionary panorama and with spectacular crowd scenes:

1° puncto. El primer puncto es ver las personas, las unas
y las otras; y primero las de la haz de la tierra, en tanta
diversidad, así en trajes como en gestos, unos blancos y
otros negros, unos en paz y otros en guerra, unos llorando
y otros riendo, unos sanos, otros enfermos, unos nasciendo
y otros muriendo, etc.

2°: ver y considerar las tres personas divinas, como en el
su solio real o throno de la su divina majestad, cómo miran
toda la haz y redondez de la tierra y todas las gentes en
tanta ceguedad, y cómo mueren y descienden al infierno.

1st point. The first point is to see people, of this and that kind; and first of all those on the face of the earth in all their variety of garments and gestures, some white and others black, some in peace and some at war, some weeping and others laughing, some healthy and others sick, some being born and others dying, etc.

2nd: to see and to consider the three divine persons as on the regal seat or throne of their divine majesty, how they look down on the whole face and rotundity of the earth and all the people who are in such blindness, and how they die and descend to hell.

The idea that the God of Moses does not tolerate being represented in visual images does not ever seem to have occurred to Ignatius of Loyola. On the contrary, one might say that he claims for each and every Christian the grandiose visionary gifts of Dante or Michelangelo—without even the restraint that Dante seems obliged to impose on his own visual imagination when face to face with the celestial visions of Paradise.

In Loyola's spiritual exercise for the following day (second meditation), the person meditating has to put himself into the scene and assume the role of an actor in the imaginary action:

El primer puncto es ver las personas, es a saber, ver a Nuestra Señora y a Joseph y a la ancila y al niño Jesú, después de ser nascido, haciéndome yo un pobrecito y esclavito indigno, mirándolos, contemplándolos y serviéndolos en sus necessidades, como si presente me hallase, con todo acatamiento y reverencia possible; y después reflectir en mí mismo para sacar algún provecho.

The first point is to see the people concerned, that is, to see Our Lady and Joseph and the handmaiden and the Child Jesus newly born, making myself into a poor wretch, a base slave, gazing on them, contemplating them and serving their needs, as if I were present there, with all possible devotion and reverence; and thereafter to reflect upon myself, in order to obtain some profit.

Certainly Catholicism of the Counter-Reformation possessed a fundamental vehicle, in its ability to use visual communication: through the emotional stimuli of sacred art, the believer was supposed to grasp the meaning of the verbal teachings of the Church. But it was always a matter of starting from a given image, one proposed by the Church itself and not "imagined" by the believer. What I think distinguishes Loyola's procedure, even with regard to the forms of devotion of his own time, is the shift from the word to the visual image as a way of attaining knowledge of the most profound meaning. Here too the point of departure and the point of arrival are already established, but in the middle there opens up a field of infinite possibilities in the application of the individual imagination, in how one depicts characters, places, and scenes in motion. The believer is called upon personally to paint frescoes crowded with figures on the walls of his mind, starting out from the stimuli that his visual imagination succeeds in extracting from a theological proposition or a laconic verse from the gospels.

Let us return to purely literary problematics and ask ourselves about the genesis of the imaginary at a time when literature no longer refers back to an authority or a tradition as its origin or goal, but aims at novelty, originality, and invention. It seems to me that in this situation the question of the priority of the visual image or verbal expression (which is rather like the problem of the chicken and the egg) tends definitely to lean toward the side of the visual imagination.

Where do they come from, these images that rain down into the fantasy? Dante, justifiably, had a high opinion of himself, to the point of having no scruples about proclaiming the direct divine inspiration of his visions. Writers closer to us in time (with the exception of those few cases of prophetic vocation) establish their contacts through earthly transmitters, such as the individual or the collective unconscious; the time regained in feelings that reemerges from time lost; or "epiphanies," concentrations of being in a single spot or point of time. In short, it is a question of processes that, even if they do not originate in the heavens, certainly go beyond our intentions and our control, acquiring—with respect to the individual—a kind of transcendence.

Nor is it only poets and novelists who deal with this problem. A specialist on the nature of intelligence, Douglas Hofstadter, does a similar thing in his famous book *Gödel, Escher, Bach,* in which the real problem is the choice between various images that have rained down into the fantasy:

> Think, for instance, of a writer who is trying to convey certain ideas which to him are contained in mental images. He isn't quite sure how those images fit together in his mind, and he experiments around, expressing things first one way and then another, and finally settles on some version. But does he know where it all came from? Only in a vague sense. Much of the source, like an iceberg, is deep underwater, unseen—and he knows that. (Vintage edition, 1980, p. 713)

But perhaps we should first to take a look at how this problem has been posed in the past. The most exhaustive, comprehensive, and clear history of the idea of imagination I have found is an essay by Jean Starobinski, "The Empire of the Imaginary" (included in the volume *La relation critique,* 1970). From the Renaissance magic of the neo-Platonists originates the idea of the imagination as a communication with the world soul, an idea that was to recur in romanticism and surrealism. This notion contrasts with that of the imagination as an instrument of knowledge, according to which the imagination, while following channels other than those of scientific knowledge, can coexist with the latter and even assist it, indeed be a phase the scientist needs in order to formulate his hypotheses. On the other hand, theories of the imagination as a depository of the truths of the universe can agree with a *Naturphilosophie* or with a kind of theosophical knowledge, but are incompatible with scientific knowledge—unless we divide what can be known into two parts, leaving the external world to science and isolating imaginative knowledge in the inner self of the individual. It is this second attitude that Starobinski recognizes as the method of Freudian analysis, while Jung's method, which bestows universal validity on archetypes and the collective unconscious, is linked to the idea of imagination as participation in the truth of the world.

At this point, there is a question I cannot evade: in which of the two tendencies outlined by Starobinski would I place my own idea of the imagination? To answer that question I am forced to look back at my own experience as a writer, and especially at the part that has to do with "fantastic" narrative writing. When I began to write fantastic stories, I did not yet consider theoretical questions; the only thing I knew was that there was a visual image at the source of all my stories. One of these images was a man cut in two halves, each of which went on living independently. Another example was a boy who climbs a tree and then makes his way from tree to tree without ever coming down to earth. Yet another was an empty suit of armor that moves and speaks as if someone were inside.

In devising a story, therefore, the first thing that comes to my mind is an image that for some reason strikes me as charged with meaning, even if I cannot formulate this meaning in discursive or conceptual terms. As soon as the image has become sufficiently clear in my mind, I set about developing it into a story; or better yet, it is the images themselves that develop their own implicit potentialities, the story they carry within them. Around each image others come into being, forming a field of analogies, symmetries, confrontations. Into the organization of this material, which is no longer purely visual but also conceptual, there now enters my deliberate intent to give order and sense to the development of the story; or rather, what I do is try to establish which meanings might be compatible with the overall design I wish to give the story and which meanings are not compatible, always leaving a certain margin of possible alternatives. At the same time, the writing, the verbal product, acquires increasing importance. I would say that from the moment I start putting black on white, what really matters is the written word, first as a search for an equivalent of the visual image, then as a coherent development of the initial stylistic direction. Finally, the written word little by little comes to dominate the field. From now on it will be the writing that guides the story toward the most felicitous verbal expression, and the visual imagination has no choice but to tag along.

In *Cosmicomics* (1965) the procedure was a little different, since the point of departure was a statement taken from the language of science; the independent play of the visual images had to arise from this conceptual statement. My aim was to show that writing using images typical of myth can grow from any soil, even from language farthest away from any visual image, as the language of science is today. Even in reading the most technical scientific book or the most abstract book of philosophy, one can come across a phrase that unexpectedly stimulates the visual imagination. We are therefore in one of those situations where the image is determined by a preexistent written text (a page or a single sentence that I come across in my reading), and from this may spring an imaginative process that might either be in the spirit of the text or go off in a direction all its own.

The first cosmicomic I wrote, "The Distance of the Moon," is possibly the most "surrealistic," in the sense that the impulse, derived from gravitational physics, leaves the door open to a dreamlike fantasy. In other cosmicomics the plot is guided by an idea more in keeping with the scientific point of departure, but always clad in a shell of imagination and feeling, and spoken by either one voice or two. In short, my procedure aims at uniting the spontaneous generation of images and the intentionality of discursive thought. Even when the opening gambit is played by the visual imagination, putting its own intrinsic logic to work, it finds itself sooner or later caught in a web where reasoning and verbal expression also impose their logic. Yet the visual solutions continue to be determining factors and sometimes unexpectedly come to decide situations that neither the conjectures of thought nor the resources of language would be capable of resolving.

One point to be cleared up about anthropomorphism in *Cosmicomics:* although science interests me just because of its efforts to escape from anthropomorphic knowledge, I am nonetheless convinced that our imagination cannot be anything *but* anthropomorphic. This is the reason for my anthropomorphic treatment of a universe in which man has never existed, and I would add that it seems extremely unlikely that man could ever exist in such a universe.

The time has come for me to answer the question I put to myself regarding Starobinski's two modes of thought: imagination as an instrument of knowledge or as identification with the world soul. Which do I choose? From what I have said, I ought to be a determined supporter of the first tendency, since for me the story is the union of a spontaneous logic of images and a plan carried out on the basis of a rational intention. But, at the same time, I have always sought out in the imagination a means to attain a knowledge that is outside the individual, outside the subjective. It is right, then, for me to declare myself closer to the second position, that of identification with the world soul.

Still there is another definition in which I recognize myself fully, and that is the imagination as a repertory of what is potential, what is hypothetical, of what does not exist and has never existed, and perhaps will never exist but might have existed. In Starobinski's treatment of the subject, this comes up when he mentions Giordano Bruno. According to Bruno, the *spiritus phantasticus* is "mundus quidem et sinus inexplebilis formarum et specierum," that is, a world or a gulf, never saturable, of forms and images. So, then, I believe that to draw on this gulf of potential multiplicity is indispensable to any form of knowledge. The poet's mind, and at a few decisive moments the mind of the scientist, works according to a process of association of images that is the quickest way to link and to choose between the infinite forms of the possible and the impossible. The imagination is a kind of electronic machine that takes account of all possible combinations and chooses the ones that are appropriate to a particular purpose, or are simply the most interesting, pleasing, or amusing.

I have yet to explain what part the *indirect* imaginary has in this gulf of the fantastic, by which I mean the images supplied by culture, whether this be mass culture or any other kind of tradition. This leads to another question: What will be the future of the individual imagination in what is usually called the "civilization of the image"? Will the power of evoking images of things that are *not there* continue to develop in a human race increasingly inundated by a flood of prefabricated images? At one time the visual memory of an individual was limited to the heritage of his direct experiences and to a restricted repertory of images reflected in culture. The possibility of giving form to personal myths arose from the way in which the fragments of this memory came together in unexpected and evocative combinations. We are bombarded today by such a quantity of images that we can no longer distinguish direct experience from what we have seen for a few seconds on television. The memory is littered with bits and pieces of images, like a rubbish dump, and it is more and more unlikely that any one form among so many will succeed in standing out.

If I have included visibility in my list of values to be saved, it is to give warning of the danger we run in losing a basic human faculty: the power of bringing visions into focus with our eyes shut, of bringing forth forms and colors from the lines of black letters on a white page, and in fact of *thinking* in terms of images. I have in mind some possible pedagogy of the imagination that would accustom us to control our own inner vision without suffocating it or letting it fall, on the other hand, into confused, ephemeral daydreams, but would enable the images to crystallize into a well-defined, memorable, and self-sufficient form, the *icastic* form.

This is of course a kind of pedagogy that we can only exercise upon ourselves, according to methods invented for the occasion and with unpredictable results. In my own early development, I was already a child of the "civilization of images," even if this was still in its infancy and a far cry from the inflations of today. Let us say that I am a product of an intermediate period, when the colored illustrations that were our childhood companions, in books, weekly magazines, and toys, were very important to us. I think that being born during that period made a profound mark on my development. My imaginary world was first influenced by the illustrations in the *Corriere dei piccoli,* the most widely circulated weekly for children. I am speaking of my life between three and thirteen years of age, before a passion for the cinema became an absolute obsession, one that lasted all through my adolescence. In fact I believe that the really vital time was between three and six, before I learned to read.

In Italy in the twenties the *Corriere dei piccoli* used to publish the best-known American comic strips of the time: Happy Hooligan, the Katzenjammer Kids, Felix the Cat, Maggie and Jiggs, all of them rebaptized with Italian names. And there were also Italian comic strips, some of them of excellent quality, according to the graphic taste and style of the period. In Italy they had not yet started to use balloons for dialogue (these began in the thirties with the importation of Mickey Mouse). The *Corriere dei piccoli* redrew the American cartoons without balloons, replacing them with two or four rhymed lines under each cartoon. However, being unable to read, I could easily dispense with the words— the pictures were enough. I used to live with this little magazine, which my mother had begun buying and collecting even before I was born and had bound into volumes year by year. I would spend hours following the cartoons of each series from one issue to another, while in my mind I told myself the stories, interpreting the scenes in different ways—I produced variants, put together the single episodes into a story of broader scope, thought out and isolated and then connected the recurring elements in each series, mixing up one series with another, and invented new series in which the secondary characters became protagonists.

When I learned to read, the advantage I gained was minimal. Those simple-minded rhyming couplets provided no illuminating information; often they were stabs in the dark like my own, and it was evident that the rhymster had no idea of what might have been in the balloons of the original, either because he did not understand English or because he was working from cartoons that had already been redrawn and rendered wordless. In any case, I preferred to ignore the written lines and to continue with my favorite occupation of daydreaming *within* the pictures and their sequence.

This habit undeniably caused a delay in my ability to concentrate on the written word, and I acquired the attention needed for reading only at a later stage and with effort. But reading the pictures without words was certainly a schooling in fable-making, in stylization, in the composition of the image. For example, the elegant way in which Pat O'Sullivan could draw the background in a little, square cartoon showing the black silhouette of Felix the Cat on a road that lost itself in a landscape beneath a full moon in a black sky: I think that has remained an ideal for me.

The work I did later in life, extracting stories from the mysterious figures of the tarot and interpreting the same figure in a different way each time, certainly had its roots in my obsessive porings over pages and pages of cartoons when I was a child. What I was trying to do in *The Castle of Crossed Destinies* (*Il castello dei destini incrociati*) is a kind of "fantastic iconology," not only with the tarot but also with great paintings. In fact I attempted to interpret the paintings of Carpaccio in San Giorgio degli Schiavoni in Venice, following the cycles of St. George and St. Jerome as if they were one story, the life of a single person, and to identify my own life with that of this George-Jerome. This fantastic iconology has become my habitual way of expressing my love of painting. I have adopted the method of telling my own stories, starting from pictures famous in the history of art or at any rate pictures that have made an impact on me.

Let us say that various elements concur in forming the visual part of the literary imagination: direct observation of the real world, phantasmic and oneiric transfiguration, the figurative world as it is transmitted by culture at its various levels, and a process of abstraction, condensation, and interiorization of sense experience, a matter of prime importance to both the visualization and the verbalization of thought. All these features are to some extent to be found in the authors I acknowledge as models, above all at those times particularly favorable to the visual imagination—that is, in the literatures of the Renaissance, the Baroque, and the Romantic age. In an anthology that I compiled of nineteenth-century fantastic tales, I followed the visionary and spectacular vein that pulses in the stories of Hoffmann, Chamisso, Arnim, Eichendorff, Potocki, Gogol, Nerval, Gautier, Hawthorne, Poe, Dickens, Turgenev, Leskov, and continues down to Stevenson, Kipling, and Wells. And along with this I followed another, sometimes in the very same authors: the vein that makes fantastic events spring from the everyday—an inner, mental, invisible fantasy, culminating in Henry James.

Will the literature of the fantastic be possible in the twenty-first century, with the growing inflation of prefabricated images? Two paths seem to be open from now on. (1) We could recycle used images in a new context that changes their meaning. Postmodernism may be seen as the tendency to make ironic use of the stock images of the mass media, or to inject the taste for the marvelous inherited from literary tradition into narrative mechanisms that accentuate its alienation. (2) We could wipe the slate clean and start from scratch. Samuel Beckett has obtained the most extraordinary results by reducing visual and linguistic elements to a minimum, as if in a world after the end of the world.

Perhaps the first text in which all these problems are present at the same time is Balzac's *Le chef-d'oeuvre inconnu* (The Unknown

Masterpiece). And it is no coincidence that what we may call a prophetic insight came from Balzac, situated as he was at a nodal point in the history of literature, in a liminal experience, now visionary and now realistic, now both together—always apparently drawn by the forces of nature, though always very much aware of what he was doing.

Le chef-d'oeuvre inconnu, on which he worked from 1831 to 1837, at first carried the subtitle of "conte fantastique," while in the final version it figures as an "étude philosophique." What happened in between was that—as Balzac himself puts it in another story—literature had killed the fantastic. In the first version of the story (published in a magazine in 1831), the elderly painter Frenhofer's perfect picture, in which only a woman's foot emerges from a chaos of color, from a shapeless fog, is both understood and admired by the artist's two colleagues, Pourbus and Nicholas Poussin: "Combien de jouissances sur ce morceau de toile!" (How many delights on this small piece of canvas!). And even the model, who does not understand it, is nonetheless impressed in some way.

In the second version, still 1831 but in book form, a few added scraps of conversation reveal the incomprehension of Frenhofer's colleagues. He is still an inspired mystic who lives for his ideal, but he is condemned to solitude. The final version (1837) adds many pages of technical reflection on painting, and an ending that makes it clear that Frenhofer is a madman doomed to lock himself up with his supposed masterpiece, then to burn it and commit suicide.

Le chef-d'oeuvre inconnu has often been commented on as a parable of modern art. Reading the latest of these studies, by Hubert Damisch (in *Fenêtre jaune cadmium,* 1984), I realized that the story can also be read as a parable of literature, about the unbridgeable gulf between linguistic expression and sense experience, and the elusiveness of the visual imagination. Balzac's first version contains a definition of the fantastic as indefinable: "Pour toutes ces singularités, l'idiome moderne n'a qu'un mot: *c'était indefinissable* . . . Admirable expression. Elle résume la littérature fantastique; elle dit tout ce qui échappe aux perceptions bornées de notre esprit; et quand vous l'avez placées sous les yeux d'un lecteur, il est lancé dans l'espace imaginaire" (For all these remarkable things, modern idiom has but the one word: *it was indefinable* . . . An admirable expression. It sums up the literature of the fantastic; it says everything that eludes the limited perceptions of our spirit; and when you have placed it before the eyes of a reader, he is launched into imaginary space).

In the years that followed, Balzac rejected the literature of fantasy, which for him had meant art as the mystical knowledge of everything, and turned to the minute description of the world as it is, still convinced that he was expressing the secret of life. Just as Balzac himself was for a long time uncertain whether to make Frenhofer into a seer or a madman, so his story continues to contain an ambiguity in which its deepest truth resides. The artist's imagination is a world of potentialities that no work will succeed in realizing. What we experience by living is another world, answering to other forms of order and disorder. The layers of words that accumulate on the page, like the layers of colors on the canvas, are yet another world, also infinite but more easily controlled, less refractory to formulation. The link between the three worlds is the *indefinable* spoken of by Balzac: or, rather, I would call it the *undecidable,* the paradox of an infinite whole that contains other infinite wholes.

A writer—and I am speaking of a writer of infinite ambitions, like Balzac—carries out operations that involve the infinity of his imagination or the infinity of the contingency that may be attempted, or both, by means of the infinity of linguistic possibilities in writing. Some might object that a single lifetime, from birth to death, can contain only a finite amount of information. How can the individual's stock of images and individual experience extend beyond that limit? Well, I believe that these attempts to escape the vortex of multiplicity are useless. Giordano Bruno explained to us that the *spiritus phantasticus* from which the writer's imagination draws forms and figures is a bottomless well; and as for external reality, Balzac's *Comédie humaine* starts from the assumption that the written world can be homologous to the living world, not only that of today but also of yesterday or tomorrow.

As a writer of fantasy, Balzac tried to capture the world soul in a single symbol among the infinite number imaginable; but to do this he was forced to load the written word with such intensity that it would have ended by no longer referring to a world outside its own self, like the colors and lines in Frenhofer's picture. When he reached this threshold, Balzac stopped and changed his whole program: no longer intensive but extensive writing. Balzac the realist would try through writing to embrace the infinite stretch of space and time, swarming with multitudes, lives, and stories.

But could it not happen as it does in Escher's pictures, which Douglas Hofstadter cites as an illustration of Gödel's paradox? In a gallery of paintings, a man is looking at the landscape of a city, and this landscape opens up to embrace the gallery that contains it and the man who is looking at it. In his infinite *Comédie humaine* Balzac should also have included the writer of fantasy that he was or had been, with all his infinite fantasies; and he should have included the realistic writer that he was or wanted to be, intent on capturing the infinite real world in his "human comedy." (Though maybe it is the infinite inner world of Balzac the fantasist that includes the inner world of Balzac the realist, because one of the infinite fantasies of the former coincides with the realistic infinity of the *Comédie humaine* . . . . .)

Still, all "realities" and "fantasies" can take on form only by means of writing, in which outwardness and innerness, the world and I, experience and fantasy, appear composed of the same verbal material. The polymorphic visions of the eyes and the spirit are contained in uniform lines of small or capital letters, periods, commas, parentheses—pages of signs, packed as closely together as grains of sand, representing the many-colored spectacle of the world on a surface that is always the same and always different, like dunes shifted by the desert wind.

5

MULTIPLICITY

Let us begin with a quotation, from the novel *That Awful Mess on the Via Merulana* by Carlo Emilio Gadda:

"Nella sua saggezza e nella sua povertà molisana, il dottor Ingravallo, che pareva vivere di silenzio e di sonno sotto la giungla nera di quella parrucca, lucida come pece e riccioluta come d'agnello d'Astrakan, nella sua saggezza interrompeva talora codesto sonno e silenzio per enunciare qualche teoretica idea (idea generale s'intende) sui casi degli uomini: e delle donne. A prima vista, cioè al primo udirle, sembravano banalità. Non erano banalità. Così quei rapidi enunciati, che facevano sulla sua bocca il crepitio improvviso d'uno zolfanello illuminatore, rivivevano poi nei timpani della gente a distanza di ore, o di mesi, dalla enunciazione: come dopo un misterioso tempo incubatorio. 'Già!' riconosceva l'interessato: 'il dottor Ingravallo me l'aveva pur detto.' Sosteneva, fra l'altro, che le inopinate catastrofi non sono mai la conseguenza o l'effetto che dir si voglia d'un unico motivo, d'una causa al singolare: ma sono come un vortice, un punto di depressione ciclonica nella coscienza del mondo, verso cui hanno cospirato tutta una molteplicità di causali convergenti. Diceva anche nodo o groviglio, o garbuglio, o gnommero, che alla romana vuol dire gomitolo. Ma il termine giuridico 'le causali, la causale' gli sfuggiva preferentemente di bocca: quasi contro sua voglia. L'opinione che bisognasse 'riformare in noi il senso della catego-

ria di causa' quale avevamo dai filosofi, da Aristotele o da Em-
manuele Kant, e sostituire alla causa le cause era in lui una opinione centrale e persistente: una fissazione, quasi: che gli
evaporava dalle labbra carnose, ma piuttosto bianche, dove un
mozzicone di sigaretta spenta pareva, pencolando da un angolo,
accompagnare la sonnolenza dello sguardo e il quasi-ghigno, tra
amaro e scettico, a cui per 'vecchia' abitudine soleva atteggiare
la metà inferiore della faccia, sotto quel sonno della fronte e delle
palpebre e quel nero pìceo della parrucca. Così, proprio così,
avveniva dei 'suoi' delitti. 'Quanno me chiammeno! . . . Già. Si
me chiammeno a me . . . può sta ssicure ch'è nu guaio: quacche
gliuommero . . . de sberretà . . . ' diceva, contaminando napoli-
tano, molisano, e italiano.

"La causale apparente, la causale principe, era sì, una. Ma il
fattaccio era l'effetto di tutta una rosa di causali che gli eran
soffiate addosso a molinello (come i sedici venti della rosa dei
venti quando s'avviluppano a tromba in una depressione ciclonica) e avevano finito per strizzare nel vortice del delitto la de-
bilitata 'ragione del mondo.' Come si storce il collo a un pollo. E
poi soleva dire, ma questo un po' stancamente, 'ch'i' femmene se
retroveno addo' n'i vuò truvà.' Una, tarda riedizione italica del
vieto 'cherchez la femme.' E poi pareva pentirsi, come d'aver
calunniato 'e femmene, e voler mutare idea. Ma allora si sarebbe
andati nel difficile. Sicché taceva pensieroso, come temendo d'a-
ver detto troppo. Voleva significare che un certo movente affet-
tivo, un tanto o, direste oggi, un quanto di affettività, un certo
'quanto di erotia,' si mescolava anche ai 'casi d'interesse,' ai delitti
apparentemente più lontani dalle tempeste d'amore. Qualche
collega un tantino invidioso delle sue trovate, qualche prete più
edotto dei molti danni del secolo, alcuni subalterni, certi uscieri,
i superiori, sostenevano che leggesse dei libri strani: da cui cavava
tutte quelle parole che non vogliono dir nulla, o quasi nulla, ma

servono come non altre ad accileccare gli sprovveduti, gli ignari.
Erano questioni un po' da manicomio: una terminologia da me-
dici dei matti. Per la pratica ci vuol altro! I fumi e le filosoficherie
son da lasciare ai trattatisti: la pratica dei commissariati e della
squadra mobile è tutt'un altro affare: ci vuole della gran pazienza,
della gran carità: uno stomaco pur anche a posto: e, quando non
traballi tutta la baracca dei taliani, senso di responsabilità e de-
cisione sicura, moderazione civile; già: già: e polso fermo. Di
queste obiezioni così giuste lui, don Ciccio, non se ne dava per
inteso: seguitava a dormire in piedi, a filosofare a stomaco vuoto,
e a fingere di fumare la sua mezza sigheretta, regolarmente
spenta."

"In his wisdom and in his Molisan poverty, Officer Ingravallo,
who seemed to live on silence and sleep under the black jungle
of that mop, shiny as pitch and curly as astrakhan lamb, in his
wisdom, he sometimes interrupted this silence and this sleep to
enunciate some theoretical idea (a general idea, that is) on the
affairs of men, and of women. At first sight, or rather, on first
hearing, these seemed banalities. They weren't banalities. And so,
those rapid declarations, which crackled on his lips like the sudden illumination of a sulphur match, were revived in the ears of
people at a distance of hours, or of months, from their enuncia-
tion: as if after a mysterious period of incubation. 'That's right!'
the person in question admitted, 'That's exactly what Ingravallo
said to me.' He sustained, among other things, that unforeseen
catastrophes are never the consequence or the effect, if you prefer, of a single motive, of *a* cause singular; but they are rather
like a whirlpool, a cyclonic point of depression in the consciousness of the world, towards which a whole multitude of converg-
ing causes have contributed. He also used words like knot or
tangle, or muddle, or *gnommero,* which in Roman dialect means

skein. But the legal term, 'the motive, the motives,' escaped his
lips by preference, though as if against his will. The opinion that
we must "reform within ourselves the meaning of the category
of cause," as handed down by the philosophers from Aristotle to
Immanuel Kant, and replace cause with causes was for him a
central, persistent opinion, almost a fixation, which melted from
his fleshy, but rather white lips, where the stub of a spent ciga-
rette seemed, dangling from one corner, to accompany the som-
nolence of his gaze and the quasi-grin, half-bitter, half-skeptical,
in which through 'old' habit he would fix the lower half of his
face beneath that sleep of his forehead and eyelids and that pitchy
black of his mop. This was how, exactly how he defined 'his'
crimes. 'When they call me . . . Sure. If they call *me,* you can
be sure that there's trouble: some mess, some *gliuommero* to un-
tangle,' he would say, garbling his Italian with the dialects of
Naples and the Molise.

"The apparent motive, the principal motive was, of course,
single. But the crime was the effect of a whole list of motives
which had blown on it in a whirlwind (like the sixteen winds in
the list of winds when they twist together in a tornado, in a
cyclonic depression) and had ended by pressing into the vortex
of the crime the enfeebled 'reason of the world.' Like wringing
the neck of a chicken. And then he used to say, but this a bit
wearily, 'you're sure to find skirts where you don't want to find
them.' A belated Italian revision of the trite *'cherchez la femme.'*
And then he seemed to repent, as if he had slandered the ladies,
and wanted to change his mind. But that would have got him
into difficulties. So he would remain silent and pensive, afraid he
had said too much. What he meant was that a certain affective
motive, a certain amount or, as you might say today, a quantum
of affection, of 'eros,' was also involved even in 'matters of interest,' in crimes which were apparently far removed from the tem-

pests of love. Some colleagues, a tiny bit envious of his intuitions, a few priests, more acquainted with the many evils of our times, some subalterns, clerks, and his superiors too, insisted he read strange books: from which he drew all those words that mean nothing, or almost nothing, but which serve better than others to dazzle the naive, the ignorant. His terminology was for doctors in looneybins. But practical action takes something else! Notions and philosophizing are to be left to scribblers: the practical experience of the police stations and the homicide squad is quite another thing: it takes plenty of patience, and charity, and a strong stomach; and when the whole shooting match of the Italians isn't tottering, a sense of responsibility, prompt decision, civil moderation: yes, yes, and a firm hand. On him, on Don Ciccio, these objections, just as they were, had no effect; he continued to sleep on his feet, philosophize on an empty stomach, and pretend to smoke his half-cigarette which had, always, gone out."*

I wished to begin with this passage from Gadda because it seems to me an excellent introduction to the subject of my lecture—which is the contemporary novel as an encyclopedia, as a method of knowledge, and above all as a network of connections between the events, the people, and the things of the world.

I could have chosen other novelists to exemplify this "calling" so typical of the present century. I chose Gadda because he wrote in my own language and is relatively little known in the United States (partly because of the particular complexity of his style, difficult even in Italian); also because his philosophy fits in very well with my theme, in that he views the world as a "system of

---

Quer pasticciaccio brutto de via Merulana (Milan: Garzanti, 1957); *That Awful Mess on Via Merulana,* translated by William Weaver (New York: George Braziller, 1965), pp. 4–6.

systems," where each system conditions the others and is conditioned by them.

Carlo Emilio Gadda tried all his life to represent the world as a knot, a tangled skein of yarn; to represent it without in the least diminishing the inextricable complexity or, to put it better, the simultaneous presence of the most disparate elements that converge to determine every event. He was led to this vision of things by his intellectual training, his temperament as a writer, and his neuroses. As an engineer, Gadda was brought up on the culture of science, equipped with technical know-how and a positive fervor for philosophy. The last of these, incidentally—his passion for philosophy—he kept a secret: it was only among the papers discovered after his death in 1973 that we learned of his rough draft for a philosophical system based on Spinoza and Leibniz. As a writer—thought of as the Italian equivalent to James Joyce—Gadda developed a style to match his complicated epistemology, in that it superimposes various levels of language, high and low, and uses the most varied vocabulary. As a neurotic, Gadda throws the whole of himself onto the page he is writing, with all his anxieties and obsessions, so that often the outline is lost while the details proliferate and fill up the whole picture. What is supposed to be a detective novel is left without a solution. In a sense, all his novels are unfinished or left as fragments, like the ruins of ambitious projects that nevertheless retain traces of the splendor and meticulous care with which they were conceived.

To get an idea of how Gadda's "encyclopedism" works in terms of a finished structure, we should turn to shorter texts, as for example his recipe for "Risotto alla Milanese," which is a masterpiece of Italian prose and practical advice in its descriptions of the grains of rice still partly in their husks ("pericarps," as he calls them), the most appropriate casseroles to use, the saffron, and the successive phases of cooking. Another text is devoted to building techniques where the use of prestressed concrete and hollow bricks no longer isolates houses either from heat or from noise. There follows a grotesque description both of his life in a modern building and of his obsession with all the noises that assault his ears.

In these brief pieces, as in each episode in one of Gadda's novels, the least thing is seen as the center of a network of relationships that the writer cannot restrain himself from following, multiplying the details so that his descriptions and digressions become infinite. Whatever the starting point, the matter in hand spreads out and out, encompassing ever vaster horizons, and if it were permitted to go on further and further in every direction, it would end by embracing the entire universe.

The best example of this web radiating out from every object is the episode of finding the stolen jewels in chapter nine of *That Awful Mess*. We are told about every single precious stone, its geological history, its chemical composition, with historical and artistic references and all the possible uses to which it might be put, together with the associations of images that these evoke. The most important critical essay on the epistemology implicit in Gadda's writing, Gian Carlo Roscioni's "La disarmonia prestabilita" (Deliberate Disharmony), begins with an analysis of those five pages on gems. Starting from there, Roscioni explains how for Gadda this knowledge of things—seen as the convergence of infinite relationships, past and future, real or possible—demands that everything should be precisely named, described, and located in space and time. He does this by exploiting the semantic potential of words, of all the varieties of verbal and syntactical forms with their connotations and tones, together with the often comic effects created by their juxtaposition.

A grotesque drollery with moments of frenzied desperation is characteristic of Gadda's vision. Even before science had officially recognized that observation intervenes in some way to modify the phenomenon being observed, Gadda knew that "conoscere è inserire alcunchè nel reale; e, quindi, deformare il reale" (to know is to insert something into what is real, and hence to distort reality). From this arises his invariably distorting way of representing things, and the tension he always establishes between himself and the thing represented, so that the more the world becomes distorted before his eyes, the more the author's self becomes involved in this process and is itself distorted and confused.

The passion for knowledge therefore carries Gadda from the objectivity of the world to his own irritated subjectivity, and this—for a man who does not like himself, and indeed detests himself—is a fearful torture, as is abundantly demonstrated in his novel *La cognizione del dolore* (Acquainted with Grief). In this most autobiographical of his books, Gadda explodes into a furious invective against the pronoun "I" and indeed against all pronouns, those parasites of thought: "l'io, io! . . . il più lurido di tutti i pronomi! . . . I pronomi! Sono i pidocchi del pensiero. Quando il pensiero ha i pidocchi, si gratta come tutti quelli che hanno i pidocchi . . . e nelle unghie, allora . . . ci ritrova i pronomi: i pronomi di persona" (I, I! . . . the filthiest of all the pronouns! . . . The pronouns! They are the lice of thought. When a thought has lice, it scratches, like everyone with lice . . . and in your fingernails, then . . . you find pronouns: the personal pronouns).

If Gadda's writing is determined by this tension between rational exactitude and frenetic distortion as basic components of every cognitive process, during the same period another writer with a technical-scientific training, Robert Musil, also an engineer, expressed the tension between mathematical exactitude and the imprecision of human affairs, employing a completely different kind of writing: fluent, ironic, and controlled. Musil's dream was of a mathematics of single solutions:

> Aber er hatte noch etwas auf der Zunge gehabt; etwas von mathematischen Aufgaben, die keine allgemeine Lösung zulassen, wohl aber Einzellösungen, durch deren Kombination man sich der allgemeinen Lösung nähert. Er hätte hinzufügen können, dass er die Aufgabe des menschlichen Lebens für eine solche ansah. Was man ein Zeitalter nennt—ohne zu wissen, ob man Jahrhunderte, Jahrtausende oder die Spanne zwischen Schule und Enkelkind darunter verstehen soll—dieser breite, ungeregelte Fluss von Zuständen würde dann ungefähr ebensoviel bedeuten wie ein planloses Nacheinander von ungenügenden und einzeln genommen falschen Lösungsversuchen, aus denen, erst wenn die Menschheit sie zusammenzufassen verstünde, die richtige und totale Lösung hervorgehen könnte.
> In der Strassenbahn erinnerte er sich auf dem Heimweg daran. (*Der Mann ohne Eigenschaften,* I.358)

> But there was something else he also had had on the tip of his tongue, something about mathematical problems that did not admit of any general solution, though they did admit of particular solutions, the combination of which could bring one closer to the general solution. He might have added that he regarded the problem set by every human life as one of these. What someone calls an age—without knowing whether he should by that understand centuries, millennia, or the span of time between schooldays and grandparenthood—this broad, unregulated flux of

conditions would then amount to much the same thing as a chaotic succession of unsatisfactory and, when taken singly, false attempts at a solution, attempts that might produce the correct and total solution, but only after men had learned to combine them.

In the tram going home he remembered this.

For Musil, knowledge is the awareness of the incompatibility of two opposite polarities. One of these he calls exactitude—or at other times mathematics, pure spirit, or even the military mentality—while the other he calls soul, or irrationality, humanity, chaos. Everything he knows or thinks he deposits in an encyclopedic book that he tries to keep in the form of a novel, but its structure continually changes; it comes to pieces in his hands. The result is that not only does he never manage to finish the novel, but he never succeeds in deciding on its general outlines or how to contain the enormous mass of material within set limits. If we compare these two engineer-writers, Gadda, for whom understanding meant allowing himself to become tangled in a network of relationships, and Musil, who gives the impression of always understanding everything in the multiplicity of codes and levels of things without ever allowing himself to become involved, we have to record this one fact common to both: their inability to find an ending.

Not even Marcel Proust managed to put an end to his encyclopedic novel, though not for lack of design, since the idea for the book came to him all at once, the beginning and end and the general outline. The reason was that the work grew denser and denser from the inside through its own organic vitality. The network that links all things is also Proust's theme, but in him this net is composed of points in space-time occupied in succession by everyone, which brings about an infinite multiplication of the dimensions of space and time. The world expands until it can no longer be grasped, and knowledge, for Proust, is attained by suffering this intangibility. In this sense a typical experience of knowledge is the jealousy felt by the narrator for Albertine:

> Et je comprenais l'impossibilité où se heurte l'amour. Nous nous imaginons qu'il a pour objet un être qui peut être couché devant nous, enfermé dans un corps. Hélas! Il est l'extension de cet être à tous les points de l'espace et du temps que cet être a occupé et occupera. Si nous ne possédons pas son contact avec tel lieu, avec telle heure, nous ne le possédons pas. Or nous ne pouvons toucher tous ces points. Si encore ils nous étaient désignés, peut-être pourrions-nous nous étendre jusqu'à eux. Mais nous tâtonnons sans les trouver. De là la défiance, la jalousie, les persécutions. Nous perdons un temps précieux sur une piste absurde et nous passons sans le soupçonner à côté du vrai.

> And I realised the impossibility which love comes up against. We imagine that it has as its object a being that can be laid down in front of us, enclosed within a body. Alas, it is the extension of that being to all the points in space and time that it has occupied and will occupy. If we do not possess its contact with this or that place, this or that hour, we do not possess that being. But we cannot touch all these points. If only they were indicated to us, we might perhaps contrive to reach out to them. But we grope for them without finding them. Hence mistrust, jealousy, persecutions. We waste precious time on absurd clues and pass by the truth without suspecting it.*

---

*A la recherche du temps perdu: La prisonnière (Paris: Pléiade, Gallimard, 1954), III.100; Remembrance of Things Past: The Captive, translated by C. K. Moncrieff, Terence Kilmartin, and Andreas Mayor (New York: Random House, 1981), p. 95.

This passage is on the same page in *The Captive* that deals with the irascible deities who control the telephone. A few pages later we are present at one of the first displays of airplanes, as in the volume before (*Cities of the Plain*) we saw cars replacing carriages, changing the ratio of space to time to such an extent that "l'art en est aussi modifié" (art is also changed by it). I say all this to show that, in his awareness of technology, Proust does not fall short of the two engineer-writers I mentioned earlier. The advent of modern technology that we see emerging little by little in the *Remembrance* is not just part of the "color of the times," but part of the work's very form, of its inner logic, of the author's anxiety to plumb the multiplicity of the writable within the briefness of life that consumes it.

In my first lecture I started with the epic poems of Lucretius and Ovid, and with the idea of a system of infinite relationships between *everything* and *everything else* that is to be found in two such different books. In this lecture I think that references to literature of the past may be reduced to a minimum, with just a few to show that in our own times literature is attempting to realize this ancient desire to represent the multiplicity of relationships, both in effect and in potentiality.

Overambitious projects may be objectionable in many fields, but not in literature. Literature remains alive only if we set ourselves immeasurable goals, far beyond all hope of achievement. Only if poets and writers set themselves tasks that no one else dares imagine will literature continue to have a function. Since science has begun to distrust general explanations and solutions that are not sectorial and specialized, the grand challenge for literature is to be capable of weaving together the various branches of knowledge, the various "codes," into a manifold and multifaceted vision of the world.

One writer who most certainly placed no limitations on the ambitiousness of his projects was Goethe, who in 1780 confided to Charlotte von Stein that he was planning a "novel about the universe." We know next to nothing about how he intended to lend substance to this notion, but the very fact that he chose the novel as the literary form that might contain the whole universe is itself a fact laden with significance for the future. At more or less the same time, Georg Christoph Lichtenberg wrote: "I think that a poem about empty space would be sublime." The universe and the void: I shall return to these two terms, which often tend to become one and the same thing, but between which the target of literature swings back and forth.

I found these quotations from Goethe and Lichtenberg in a marvelous book by Hans Blumenberg, *Die Lesbarkeit der Welt* (The Legibility of the World, 1981). In the last few chapters the author follows the history of this literary ambition from Novalis, who sets out to write the "ultimate book," which at one moment is a sort of encyclopedia and at others a Bible, to Humboldt, who with his *Kosmos* actually achieved his aim of writing a "description of the physical universe." The chapter in Blumenberg that concerns my subject most directly is the one called "The Empty Book of the World," which deals with Mallarmé and Flaubert. I have always been fascinated by the fact that Mallarmé, who in his poems succeeded in giving a uniquely crystalline form to nothingness, devoted the last years of his life to the project of writing the Absolute Book, as the ultimate goal of the universe: a mysterious work of which he destroyed every trace. In the same way, it is fascinating to think about Flaubert, who on 16 January 1852 wrote to Louise Colet, "ce que je voudrais faire, c'est un livre sur rien" (what I'd like to do is a book about nothing), and then went on to devote the last ten years of his life to the most encyclopedic novel ever written, *Bouvard and Pécuchet*.

Bouvard and Pécuchet is truly the ancestor of the novels I shall mention this evening, even if the pathetic and exhilarating voyage through the seas of universal knowledge taken by these two Don Quixotes of nineteenth-century scientism turns out to be a series of shipwrecks. For these two self-taught innocents, each book throws open a new world, but the worlds are mutually exclusive or at least are so contradictory as to destroy any hope of certainty. However much effort they put into it, the two scriveners are lacking in the kind of subjective gift that enables one to adapt ideas to the use one wishes to put them to, or to the gratuitous pleasure that one wishes to derive from them, a gift that cannot be learned from books.

There is a question as to how we should interpret the end of this unfinished novel, with Bouvard and Pécuchet giving up the idea of understanding the world, resignation to their fate as scriveners, and the decision to devote themselves to the task of copying the books in the universal library. Should we conclude that in the experience of Bouvard and Pécuchet "encyclopedia" and "nothingness" fuse together? But behind the two characters there is Flaubert himself, who in order to nourish their adventures chapter by chapter is forced to acquire a knowledge of everything that can be known and to build up an edifice of science for his two heroes to knock down. To this end he reads manuals of agriculture and horticulture, chemistry, anatomy, medicine, geology. In a letter dated August 1873 he said that with this aim, and taking notes all the while, he had read 194 books; in June 1874 the figure had risen to 294; and five years later he was able to announce to Zola: "Mes lectures sont finies et je n'ouvre plus aucun bouquin jusqu'à la termination de mon roman" (My readings are finished and I won't open another old book until my novel is done). But in his letters shortly afterwards we find him coming to grips with ecclesiastical texts and then turning to pedagogy, a discipline that forces him to start out on the most diverse branches of knowledge. In January 1880 he wrote: "Savez-vous à combien se montent les volumes qu'il m'a fallu absorber pour mes deux bonhommes? A plus de 1500!" (Do you know how many volumes I've had to absorb on behalf of my two worthy friends? More than 1500!).

The encyclopedic epic of the two self-educated scriveners is therefore *doublée* by a parallel and absolutely titanic effort achieved in the realm of reality. It is Flaubert in person who is transforming himself into an encyclopedia of the universe, assimilating with a passion in no way inferior to that of his heroes every scrap of the knowledge that they sought to make their own, and all that they are destined to be excluded from. Did he toil so long to demonstrate the vanity of knowledge as exploited by his two self-educated heroes? ("Du défaut de méthode dans les sciences" [On Lack of Method in the Sciences] is the subtitle Flaubert wanted to give his novel, as we see from a letter of 16 December 1879.) Or was it to demonstrate the vanity of knowledge pure and simple?

An encyclopedic novelist of a century later, Raymond Queneau, wrote an essay to defend the two heroes from the accusation of *bêtise* (their crime was being "épris d'absolu," in love with the absolute, allowing no contradictions or doubts), and also to defend Flaubert of the oversimplified accusation that he was an enemy of science. "Flaubert est *pour* la science," says Queneau, "dans la mesure justement où celle-ci est sceptique, réservée, méthodique, prudente, humaine. Il a horreur des dogmatiques, des métaphysiciens, des philosophes" (Flaubert is *for* science in exactly the extent to which it is skeptical, reserved, methodical, prudent, human. He has a horror of dogmaticians, metaphysicians, and philosophers).

Flaubert's skepticism and his endless curiosity about the human knowledge accumulated over the centuries are the very qualities that were destined to be claimed for their own by the greatest writers of the twentieth century. But theirs I would tend to call an active skepticism, a kind of gambling and betting in a tireless effort to establish relationships between discourse, methods, and levels of meaning. Knowledge as multiplicity is the thread that binds together the major works both of what is called modernism and of what goes by the name of the *postmodern,* a thread—over and above all the labels attached to it—that I hope will continue into the next millennium.

Let us remember that the book many call the most complete introduction to the culture of our century is itself a novel: Thomas Mann's *Magic Mountain.* It is not too much to say that the small, enclosed world of an alpine sanatorium is the starting point for all the threads that were destined to be followed by the *maîtres à penser* of the century: all the subjects under discussion today were heralded and reviewed there.

What tends to emerge from the great novels of the twentieth century is the idea of an *open* encyclopedia, an adjective that certainly contradicts the noun *encyclopedia,* which etymologically implies an attempt to exhaust knowledge of the world by enclosing it in a circle. But today we can no longer think in terms of a totality that is not potential, conjectural, and manifold.

Medieval literature tended to produce works expressing the sum of human knowledge in an order and form of stable compactness, as in the *Commedia,* where a multiform richness of language converges with the application of a systematic and unitary mode of thought. In contrast, the modern books that we love most are the outcome of a confluence and a clash of a multiplicity of interpretative methods, modes of thought, and styles of expression. Even if the overall design has been minutely planned, what matters is not the enclosure of the work within a harmonious figure, but the centrifugal force produced by it—a plurality of languages as a guarantee of a truth that is not merely partial. This is proved by the two great writers of our century who really paid attention to the Middle Ages, T. S. Eliot and James Joyce, both of them students of Dante and both equipped with a profound consciousness of theology (though with quite different intentions). Eliot dissolves the theological pattern into the lightness of irony and in dizzying verbal magic. Joyce sets out with every intention of constructing a systematic and encyclopedic work that can be interpreted on various levels according to medieval exegetics (drawing up tables of the correspondences of the various chapters of *Ulysses* with the parts of the human body, the arts, colors, and symbols), though what he achieves above all, chapter by chapter in *Ulysses,* is an encyclopedia of styles, weaving polyphonic multiplicity into the verbal texture of *Finnegans Wake.*

It is time to put a little order into the suggestions I have put forward as examples of multiplicity. There is such a thing as the unified text that is written as the expression of a single voice, but that reveals itself as open to interpretation on several levels. Here the prize for an inventive tour-de-force goes to Alfred Jarry for *L'amour absolu* (1899), a fifty-page novel that can be read as three completely different stories: (1) the vigil of a condemned man in his cell the night before his execution; (2) the monologue of a man suffering from insomnia, who when half asleep dreams that he has been condemned to death; (3) the story of Christ. Then there is the manifold text, which replaces the oneness of a thinking "I" with a multiplicity of subjects, voices, and views of the world, on the model of what Mikhail Bakhtin has called "dialogic" or "polyphonic" or "carnivalesque," tracing its antecedents from Plato through Rabelais to Dostoevsky.

There is the type of work that, in the attempt to contain everything possible, does not manage to take on a form, to create outlines for itself, and so remains incomplete by its very nature, as we saw in the cases of Gadda and Musil.

There is the type of work that in literature corresponds to what in philosophy is nonsystematic thought, which proceeds by aphorisms, by sudden, discontinuous flashes of light; and at this point the time has come to mention an author I never tire of reading, Paul Valéry. I am speaking of his prose work composed of essays of only a few pages and notes a few lines long, found in his notebooks. "Une philosophie doit être portative" (A philosophy should be portable), he wrote (*Cahiers,* XXIV.713), but also: "J'ai cherché, je cherche et chercherai pour ce que je nomme le Phénomène Total, c'est-à-dire le Tout de la conscience, des relations, des conditions, des possibilités, des impossibilités" (I have sought, I am searching, and I will search for what I call the Total Phenomenon, that is, the Totality of conscience, relations, conditions, possibilities, and impossibilities; XII.722).

Among the values I would like passed on to the next millennium, there is this above all: a literature that has absorbed the taste for mental orderliness and exactitude, the intelligence of poetry, but at the same time that of science and of philosophy: an intelligence such as that of Valéry as an essayist and prose writer. (And if I mention Valéry in a context in which the names of novelists prevail, it is partly because, though he was not a novelist and indeed—thanks to a famous quip of his—was thought of as the official liquidator of traditional fiction, he was a critic who understood novels as no one else could, defining their specificity simply as novels.)

If I had to say which fiction writer has perfectly achieved Valéry's aesthetic ideal of exactitude in imagination and in language, creating works that match the rigorous geometry of the crystal and the abstraction of deductive reasoning, I would without hesitation say Jorge Luis Borges. The reasons for my fondness for Borges do not end here, but I will mention only the main ones. I love his work because every one of his pieces contains a model of the universe or of an attribute of the universe (infinity, the innumerable, time eternal or present or cyclic); because they are texts contained in only a few pages, with an exemplary economy of expression; because his stories often take the outer form of some genre from popular literature, a form proved by long usage, which creates almost mythical structures. As an example let us take his most vertiginous "essay" on time, "El jardín de senderos que se bifurcan" (The Garden of Forking Paths), which is presented as a spy story and includes a totally logico-metaphysical story, which in turn contains the description of an endless Chinese novel—and all this concentrated into a dozen pages.

The hypotheses on the subject of time enunciated by Borges in this story, each one contained (and virtually hidden) in a handful of lines, are as follows. First there is an idea of precise time, almost an absolute, subjective present: "reflexioné que todas las cosas le suceden a uno precisamente, precisamente ahora. Siglos de siglos y sólo en el presente ocurren los hechos; innumerables hombres en el aire, en la tierra y el mar, y todo lo que realmente pasa me pasa a mi" (I reflected that everything, to everyone, happens precisely, precisely now. Century after century, and only in the present, do things happen. There are innumerable men in the air, on land and on sea, and everything that really happens, happens to me). Then there is a notion of time as determined by the will, in which the future appears to be as irrevocable as the past; and finally the central idea of the whole story—a manifold and ramified time in which every present forks out into two futures, so as to form "una red creciente y vertiginosa de tiempos divergentes, convergentes y paralelos" (a growing and bewildering network of divergent, convergent, and parallel forms of time). This idea of infinite contemporary universes in which all possibilities are realized in all possible combinations is by no means a digression in the story, but rather the very reason why the protagonist feels authorized to carry out the absurd and abominable crime imposed on him by his spy mission, perfectly sure that this happens only in one of the universes but not in the others; and indeed that, if he commits this crime here and now, in other universes he and his victim will be able to hail each other as friends and brothers.

The scheme of the network of possibilities may be condensed into the few pages of a story by Borges, or it may be made the supporting structure of immensely long novels, in which density and concentration are present in the individual parts. But I would say that today the rule of "Keep It Short" is confirmed even by long novels, the structure of which is accumulative, modular, and combinatory.

These considerations are at the basis of what I call the "hypernovel," which I tried to exemplify in *If on a winter's night a traveler* (*Se una notte d'inverno un viaggiatore*). My aim was to give the essence of what a novel is by providing it in concentrated form, in ten beginnings; each beginning develops in very different ways from a common nucleus, and each acts within a framework that both determines and is determined. The same principle, to sample the potential multiplicity of what may be narrated, forms the basis of another of my books, *The Castle of Crossed Destinies,* which is intended to be a kind of machine for multiplying narratives that start from visual elements with many possible meanings, such as a tarot pack. My temperament prompts me to "keep it short," and such structures as these enable me to unite density of invention and expression with a sense of infinite possibilities.

Another example of the hyper-novel is *La vie mode d'emploi* (Life, Directions for Use) by Georges Perec. It is a very long novel, made up of many intersecting stories (it is no accident that its subtitle is *Romans,* in the plural), and it reawakens the pleasure of reading the great novelistic cycles of the sort Balzac wrote. In my view, this book, published in Paris in 1978, four years before the author died at the early age of forty-six, is the last real "event" in the history of the novel so far. There are many reasons for this: the plan of the book, of incredible scope but at the same time solidly finished; the novelty of its rendering; the compendium of a narrative tradition and the encyclopedic summa of things known that lend substance to a particular image of the world; the feeling of "today" that is made from accumulations of the past and the vertigo of the void; the continual presence of anguish and irony together—in a word, the manner in which the pursuit of a definite structural project and the imponderable element of poetry become one and the same thing.

The element of "puzzle" gives the novel its plot and its formal scheme. Another scheme is the cross-section view of a typical Parisian apartment house, in which the entire action takes place, one chapter to each room. There are five storeys of apartments for each of which we are told about the furnishings and fittings, the changes of ownership and the lives of the inhabitants, together with their ancestors and descendants. The plan of the building is like a bi-square of ten squares by ten, a chessboard on which Perec passes from one pigeonhole (room, chapter) to another as the knight moves in chess, but according to a scheme that enables him to land on each of the squares in turn. (So are there a hundred chapters? No, only ninety-nine. This ultra-completed book has an intentional loophole left for incompleteness.)

So much for the container of things. As for the content, Perec drew up lists of themes, divided into categories, and decided that, even if barely hinted at, one theme from each category ought to appear in each chapter, in such a way as constantly to vary the combinations according to mathematical procedures that I am not able to define, though I have no doubts as to their exactitude. (I used to visit Perec during the nine years in which he worked on the novel, but I know only a few of his secret rules.) These categories number no fewer than forty-two and include literary quotations, geographical locations, historical facts, furniture, objects, styles, colors, foodstuffs, animals, plants, minerals, and who knows what else—and I have no idea how he managed to respect all these rules, which he did even in the shortest and most compressed chapters.

In order to escape the arbitrary nature of existence, Perec, like his protagonist, is forced to impose rigorous rules and regulations on himself, even if these rules are in turn arbitrary. But the miracle is that this system of poetics, which might seem artificial and mechanical, produces inexhaustible freedom and wealth of invention. This is because it coincides with something that had been Perec's passion ever since his first novel (*Les choses,* 1965): a passion for catalogues, for the enumeration of objects, each defined both in itself and by its belonging to an epoch, a style, a society; a passion extending to menus, concert programs, diet charts, bibliographies real or imaginary.

The demon of "collectionism" is always beating its wings over Perec's pages, and of the many collections conjured up by this book the one that is most personal and "his," I would say, is a passion for the *unique,* that is, the collection of objects of which only one specimen exists. Yet a collector he was not, in life, except of words, of the data of knowledge, of things remembered. Terminological exactitude was his way of possessing things. Perec collected and gave a name to whatever comprises the uniqueness of every event, person, or thing. No one was ever more immune than Perec to the worst blight in modern writing—which is vagueness.

I would like to stress the fact that for Perec the construction of a novel according to fixed rules, to constraints, by no means limited his freedom as a storyteller, but stimulated it. It was no coincidence that Perec was the most inventive of the members of Oulipo (Workshop of Potential Literature), founded by his mentor Raymond Queneau. Many years earlier, when he was quarreling with the automatic writing of the surrealists, Queneau wrote:

Une autre bien fausse idée qui a également cours actuellement, c'est l'équivalence que l'on établit entre inspiration, exploration du subconscient et libération, entre hasard, automatisme et liberté. Or, *cette* inspiration qui consiste à obéir aveuglément à toute impulsion est en réalité un esclavage. Le classique qui écrit sa tragédie en observant un certain nombre de régles qu'il connaît est plus libre que le poète qui écrit ce qui lui passe par la tête et qui est l'esclave d'autres règles qu'il ignore.

Another very wrong idea that is also going the rounds at the moment is the equivalence that has been established between inspiration, exploration of the subconscious, and liberation, between chance, automatism, and freedom. Now this sort of inspiration, which consists in blindly obeying every impulse, is in fact slavery. The classical author who wrote his tragedy observing a certain number of known rules is freer than the poet who writes down whatever comes into his head and is slave to other rules of which he knows nothing.

I have come to the end of this apologia for the novel as a vast net. Someone might object that the more the work tends toward the multiplication of possibilities, the further it departs from that unicum which is the *self* of the writer, his inner sincerity and the discovery of his own truth. But I would answer: Who are we, who is each one of us, if not a combinatoria of experiences, information, books we have read, things imagined? Each life is an encyclopedia, a library, an inventory of objects, a series of styles, and everything can be constantly shuffled and reordered in every way conceivable.

But perhaps the answer that stands closest to my heart is something else: Think what it would be to have a work conceived from outside the *self,* a work that would let us escape the limited perspective of the individual ego, not only to enter into selves like our own but to give speech to that which has no language, to the bird perching on the edge of the gutter, to the tree in spring and the tree in fall, to stone, to cement, to plastic . . . . .

Was this not perhaps what Ovid was aiming at, when he wrote about the continuity of forms? And what Lucretius was aiming at when he identified himself with that nature common to each and every thing?

TALKING IT OVER
by Julian Barnes

Through the indelible voices of three narrators—two best friends and the woman they both love—Julian Barnes reconstructs the romantic triangle as a weapon whose edges cut like razor blades.

"An interplay of serious thought and dazzling wit.... It's moving, it's funny, it's frightening...fiction at its best."　　　　　*—The New York Times Book Review*

Fiction/Literature/0-679-73687-5

POSSESSION
by A. S. Byatt

An intellectual mystery and a triumphant love story of a pair of young scholars researching the lives of two Victorian poets.

"Gorgeously written...dazzling...a tour de force."

—The New York Times Book Review

Fiction/Literature/0-679-73590-9

THE STRANGER
by Albert Camus

Through the story of an ordinary man who unwittingly gets drawn into a senseless murder, Camus explores what he termed "the nakedness of man faced with the absurd."

Fiction/Literature/0-679-72020-0

BREAKFAST AT TIFFANY'S
AND THREE STORIES
by Truman Capote

Truman Capote created in Holly Golightly a heroine whose name has entered the American idiom and whose style is now part of the literary landscape. Holly knows that nothing bad can ever happen to you at Tiffany's; her poignancy, wit, and naïveté continue to charm.

Also included in this volume are the stories "House of Flowers," "A Diamond Guitar," and "A Christmas Memory."

"Truman Capote is the most perfect writer of my generation. He writes the best sentences word for word, rhythm upon rhythm."　　　　—Norman Mailer

Fiction/Literature/0-679-74565-3

INVISIBLE MAN
by Ralph Ellison

This searing record of a black man's journey through contemporary America reveals, in Ralph Ellison's words, "the sheer rhetorical challenge involved in communicating across our barriers of race and religion, class, color and region."

"The greatest American novel in the second half of the twentieth century...the classic representation of American black experience."　　　—R.W. B. Lewis

Fiction/Literature/0-679-72313-7

. . . .

THE SOUND AND THE FURY
by William Faulkner

The tragedy of the Compson family, featuring some of the most memorable characters in American literature: beautiful, rebellious Caddy; the manchild Benjy; haunted, neurotic Quentin; Jason, the brutal cynic; and Dilsey, their black servant.

"For range of effect, philosophical weight, originality of style, variety of characterization, humor, and tragic intensity, [Faulkner's works] are without equal in our time and country."　　　—Robert Penn Warren

Fiction/Literature/0-679-73224-1

. . . .

A ROOM WITH A VIEW
by E. M. Forster

Caught up in a world of social snobbery, Lucy Honeychurch breaks from the claustrophobic constraints of her British guardians and takes control of her own fate, finding love with a man whose free spirit reminds her of a "room with a view."

Fiction/Literature/0-679-72476-1

. . . .

THE REMAINS OF THE DAY
by Kazuo Ishiguro

A profoundly compelling portrait of the perfect English butler and of his fading, insular world in postwar England.

"One of the best books of the year."　　　—*The New York Times Book Review*

Fiction/Literature/0-679-73172-5

. . . .

THE WOMAN WARRIOR
by Maxine Hong Kingston

"A remarkable book...As an account of growing up female and Chinese-American in California, in a laundry of course, it is anti-nostalgic; it burns the fat right out of the mind. As a dream—of the 'female avenger'—it is dizzying, elemental, a poem turned into a sword."　　　—*The New York Times*

Nonfiction/Literature/0-679-72188-6

ALL THE PRETTY HORSES
by Cormac McCarthy

At sixteen, John Grady Cole finds himself at the end of a long line of Texas ranchers, cut off from the only life he has ever imagined for himself. With two companions, he sets off for Mexico on a sometimes idyllic, sometimes comic journey, to a place where dreams are paid for in blood.

"A book of remarkable beauty and strength, the work of a master in perfect command of his medium." —*Washington Post Book World*

Winner of the National Book Award for Fiction
Fiction/Literature/0-679-74439-8

. . . .

DEATH IN VENICE
AND SEVEN OTHER STORIES
by Thomas Mann

In addition to "Death in Venice" ("A story," Mann said, "of death...of the voluptuousness of doom"), this volume includes "Mario the Magician," "Disorder and Early Sorrow," "A Man and His Dog," "Felix Krull," "The Blood of the Walsungs," "Tristan," and "Tonio Kröger."

Fiction/Literature/0-679-72206-8

. . . .

LOLITA
by Vladimir Nabokov

The famous and controversial novel that tells the story of the aging Humbert Humbert's obsessive, devouring, and doomed passion for the nymphet Dolores Haze.

"The only convincing love story of our century." —*Vanity Fair*

Fiction/Literature/0-679-72316-1

. . . .

THE ENGLISH PATIENT
by Michael Ondaatje

During the final moments of World War II, four damaged people come together in a deserted Italian villa. As their stories unfold, a complex tapestry of image and emotion, recollection and observation is woven, leaving them inextricably connected by the brutal, improbable circumstances of war.

"It seduces and beguiles us with its many-layered mysteries, its brilliantly taut and lyrical prose, its tender regard for its characters." —*Newsday*

Winner of the Booker Prize
Fiction/Literature/0-679-74520-3

. . . .

MATING
by Norman Rush

A female American anthropologist of high intellect and grand passion, at loose ends in Botswana, finds love with Nelson Denoon, a charismatic intellectual who is rumored to have founded a utopian society in the Kalahari Desert.

"A complex and moving love story...breathtaking in its cunningly intertwined intellectual sweep and brio...a major novel."   —*Chicago Tribune*

Winner of the National Book Award for Fiction
Fiction/Literature/0-679-73709-X

....

SOPHIE'S CHOICE
by William Styron

A young Southerner who yearns to become a writer befriends Nathan, a tortured, brilliant Jew, and his beautiful lover, Sophie, becoming a witness to their turbulent love-hate affair and to the burdens of Sophie's unbearable secret.

"Styron's most impressive performance.,... It belongs on that small shelf reserved for American masterpieces."   —*Washington Post Book World*

Fiction/Literature/0-679-73637-9

....

WATERLAND
by Graham Swift

Set in the bleak Fen country of East Anglia and spanning some 240 years, *Waterland* is "a gothic family saga, a detective story and a philosophical meditation on the nature and uses of history" (*The New York Times*).

"Teems with energy, fertility, violence, madness...demonstrates the irrepressible, wide-ranging talent of this young British writer."

—*Washington Post Book World*

Fiction/Literature/0-679-73979-3

....

THE PASSION
by Jeanette Winterson

Intertwining the destinies of two remarkable people—the soldier Henri, for eight years Napoleon's faithful cook, and Villanelle, the red-haired daughter of a Venetian boatman—*The Passion* is "a deeply imagined and beautiful book, often arrestingly so" (*The New York Times Book Review*).

Fiction/Literature/0-679-72437-0

....